Identity Theft Secrets

Identity Theft Secrets

Exposing the Tricks of the Trade!

DALE PENN

iUniverse, Inc.
Bloomington

Identity Theft Secrets
Exposing the Tricks of the Trade!

iUniverse books may be ordered through booksellers or by contacting:

iUniverse
1663 Liberty Drive
Bloomington, IN 47403
www.iuniverse.com
1-800-Authors (1-800-288-4677)

ISBN: 978-1-4620-0859-9 (sc)
ISBN: 978-1-4620-0858-2 (ebook)
ISBN: 978-1-4620-0857-5 (dj)

Printed in the United States of America

iUniverse rev. date: 7/21/2011

Advance Praise for *Identity Theft Secrets*

"As a former magician, Dale Penn's book Identity Theft Secrets opens the curtain to reveal the deceptions and trickery of the identity thieves."

—Mari J. Frank, Esq., author of
The Complete Idiot's Guide To Recovering from Identity Theft

"A must-read book on protecting the privacy of your identity and personal information. Dale's willingness and ability to share his own experience provides great educational insight for us all."

—Sam Sarpong, Senior Vice President and Chief Financial Officer of Broadway Federal Bank

"As a former lawmaker focused on public safety issues, I know this crime and its great cost to the American economy. All households should own this book and keep it in plain sight. Run to the nearest bookstore and follow Dale Penn's advice."

—Paula Boland, three-term Assemblywoman, California State Legislature

*For all who suspect that our frantic digital
age has diminished personal privacy
and put our families, businesses, and
financial assets at risk, take heart.
You have the capacity to fight back and win.*
—Dale Penn
Los Angeles, California

Contents

Acknowledgments

There are several coconspirators in the creation and completion of any writing endeavor, and my journey is certainly no exception.

To my editing and copy team—Lisa Jordan, Beth Strahle, Irene Matias, and Amy Bell—I thank you for your red pencils and endless patience. Let's face it; any and all remaining errors are my own.

To those who encouraged me to stick with this project in the early stages—Mark Bulluck, Daniel Furukawa, Dan Haugen, Dee Krall, Michael Caffel, Bob and Michelle Humphreys, Michael Neustadt, Danny Caudillo, and Pete Hancock—you picked me up and dusted me off more than once.

To my mentors and influences, Ronald Haines, Ken Klosterman, Bill Brewe, Esq., Richard Ammerman, Jack Goldfinger, Mike Caveney, Tom Peters, Les Brown, Tom Hopkins, Daniel Pink, Mari J. Frank, Esq., Brian Corcoran, Alan Skobin, Esq., Hon. Paula Boland, Bob Rebhun,

Gideon Grunfeld, Esq., and Liz DeClifford—each of you has left a mark upon me . . . and it still hurts!

To my close friends and accountability partners—Gerry Shaltz, Joel Bauer, Hague Atkinson, Dr. Timothy Moore, Walter Johnson, Jon Kaplan, Victor Cephas, Ted and Kim Tardiff, Bruce Prosser, Earl Lucas, Richard Rutherford, Jeff and Kim Houser, Rick and Jane Kasel, Russell Jenkins, Tim Winters, Caleb Kaltenbach, Bill Ewing, David Cruz, David Miller, Pastor Dudley C. Rutherford, and my "Every Other Friday" group at Shepherd of the Hills—without your tough love, selfless input, and guidance, I'd still be lost without a road map.

To Dom, Gen, Ali, Miles (#99), and Cha Cha—my five incredibly talented children—I can only say thanks for allowing Dad to finish this book in the solitude of my office. Despite all of my time hiding in my workspace and out of town on occasion, you are objective proof that I've been home at least five times. I love you all!

Finally, to my beautiful bride, Karen. Your patience, tireless nurturing, attention to detail, and loving encouragement are constant reminders of how much I don't deserve you. I love you and cherish our life together!

Introduction

Cybercrime has surpassed illegal drug trafficking as a criminal enterprise.
—Symantec Corporation

This book is about waging an effective, thoughtful battle against the growing worldwide threat of identity theft. Our families, businesses, and credit ratings demand that we minimize our vulnerabilities and maximize our defenses.

In 2011, Javelin Strategy & Research released its annual Identity Fraud Survey Report. Previous reports indicated an upward curve in reported incidents over the previous three years. The 2011 report found that while the overall number of reported incidents trended down for the first time in many years, the actual cost to new victims had more than doubled from the year before.

Our data-rich digital world has left us vulnerable to

new threats that come with cute and clever names but are able to pack quite a punch for both the uninformed and the unprepared. Earlier Javelin reports indicated that the average fraud amount was $4,841 dollars per victim, totaling over $54 billion dollars.

Facebook, Twitter, Flickr, LinkedIn, and other social media sites can often tempt uninformed or careless users to post their date of birth, mother's maiden name, favorite pet's name, or similar personal information without considering the privacy consequences.

While good old-fashioned dumpster diving and shoulder surfing still yield excellent results for old-school criminals, the portability of our device-driven lives leaves us open to high-tech methods that target not only our desktop computers, but mobile devices too— such as our laptops, smartphones like Droid and iPhone, flash drives, and tablet computers like the iPad.

The current recession has helped to embolden desperate criminal fraudsters and opportunists. They victimize consumers of all ages with new schemes that prey on our dependence upon technology to help us lead more productive lives.

Our emerging digital frontier has given birth to new scams with strange-sounding names like phishing, pharming, vishing, spoofing, sniffing, skimming, squatting, and spimming. These inventive names are the parlance of contemporary digital-identity thieves and the investigators committed to stopping them in their tracks.

Many identity theft victims are often denied loans for homes, vehicles, or education. Thousands of victims lose job opportunities and are even arrested for crimes they did not commit.

Our personal family friend Shelly H. was once called to voluntarily drive herself down to the Beverly Hills Police Department to help assist them in "cracking a big identity-fraud case" that they were investigating. When Shelly got there, she was promptly arrested. By the time investigators determined that Shelly was innocent, she had already been booked and locked up!

Despite the media attention that the varieties of identity theft gets these days, most folks don't recognize the evolving dangers of several emerging and dangerous strains of financial fraud. Medical identity theft is a good example of one of these growing concerns. This can occur when medical records are tampered with or polluted with false information supplied by an imposter during a medical questionnaire, emergency, exam, or procedure. Imagine for a moment a medical identity theft victim being given the wrong blood type in an emergency room as a result of false or inaccurate records in the victim's medical files.

Business enterprises can minimize their exposures through employee training and awareness programs, but corporate identity fraud is growing at an alarming rate. While the judicious use of encryption technology and employee education can limit corporate exposure, the looming threat from malicious outsiders, as well as company insiders, makes constant awareness and vigilance essential for all organizations.

A recent McAfee study found that data theft and security breaches cost businesses about $1 trillion worldwide.

Criminal Minds

I'm not a law enforcement officer. I'm not a bureaucrat or a fraud investigator. I'm not even a reformed criminal. So why have I written a book about combating identity theft awareness and simple protection strategies?

I offer this information because I am an identity theft survivor who learned quite a bit from my own ordeal. For many of us, the greatest threat to our personal privacy comes from within our own family circles, business contacts, and dangerous casual acquaintances. More often than not, identity thieves wear sheep's clothing.

I'm a graduate of the school of hard knocks, because I made a mistake. I dropped my guard and allowed myself to become an identity theft target.

After my own nightmarish personal encounter with identity theft, I felt an overwhelming drive to educate, equip, and empower others to fight back against this growing crime.

Fortunately, I come armed with another powerful weapon in the fight against identity theft: an extensive financial services, insurance, and risk management background.

James Joyce once said, "A man's errors are his portals of discovery." After my experience, I agree that these wise words hold truth. I made an error, which has, in turn, led me to many great discoveries. In the following chapters, my goal is to share those discoveries with you.

As a commercial insurance broker and consultant, I have helped protect the assets of hundreds of corporations throughout the United States for more than twenty years. I serve some of the largest clients in the United States, including Fortune 500 companies.

For over twenty years, I helped acquire and protect hundreds of thousands of new clients, which translated into a profusion of insurance premiums for our firm and our network of strategic partners, including trusted companies like Transamerica, Blue Cross, and Fireman's Fund. Consequently, the deliberate abuse of insurance and the potential financial fraud that often arises are two areas with which I've grown familiar.

The corporate clients we serve are often large companies who have much to lose by choosing the wrong insurance partner. Gratefully, they've chosen to do business with us. They trust me to protect their business assets, and that's exactly what I do.

Because my job is to protect others and their assets, I feel it is my responsibility to share what I have learned about identity theft with you. Although my personal identity theft ordeal has ended, my obligation to spread the word has not.

I've spent the past several years researching identity theft and speaking to audiences across the country about this rampant crime. In my speeches, consulting, presentations, and training seminars, I tap into my professional knowledge as well as my personal victimization to help others think and act in new ways about protecting themselves.

A Crime of Illusions

Identity theft is the fastest-growing crime in the United

States, according to the Federal Citizen Information Center (FCIC). Halfway through 2010, the total number of breached records had swollen to over 350 million!

The Identity Theft Resource Center (ITRC) reported a staggering 47 percent increase in data breaches alone between 2007 and 2008. By the end of the first quarter of 2009, the ITRC also reported that more than 1,553,000 data records had already been compromised year to date.

Why do the various forms of identity theft and fraud continue to run rampant throughout the nation? Believe it or not, it all comes down to magic. Identity theft is a shadowy world teeming with trickery, illusions, and crafty deceptions.

As local law enforcement and federal agencies can attest, this secretive world of financial crime can be extremely difficult to penetrate. Anyone—and I mean *anyone*—can be deceived by these shrewd swindlers. I was fooled, and I didn't think it was possible for someone to trick me. You see, I know my fair share about illusions.

I spent several years as a working professional magician, which means I have a unique perspective on what it takes to fool and be fooled. Over the years, I have spent countless hours perfecting various sleight of hand, illusion, and misdirection techniques. That's right—I'm a magician, a prestidigitator, a "master of illusion." Although I'm hesitant to admit it, one of those tricky identity thieves beat me at my own game.

I can't believe I fell for the misdirection. My goal is to make sure that you don't.

A Magical Boy's Life

Let me take you back a few years to when I was a youngster. Not unlike most kids in the neighborhood, I played baseball, basketball, football—but what really captured my attention was magic!

I loved pulling rabbits out of hats and making beautiful bouquets of silk flowers "magically appear" (from my sleeve). I loved the attention the art form garnered, and I definitely enjoyed making a few extra bucks. After all, you can only earn so much pocket change mowing lawns and raking leaves.

For years I worked the private party, school assembly, and after-dinner circuits with my full stage show. The routines were designed to delight, amuse, and deceive. My act consisted of mysterious and brightly colored production boxes and silk hankies, playing cards that appeared from thin air, flapping white doves guaranteed to draw a gasp, and, of course, the perfectly pressed tuxedo.

During my college years in Cincinnati, I appeared on the local CBS affiliate WCPO-TV as the Storybook Magician for a popular daily children's program called *The Uncle Al Show*. My job was to pop out of a storybook (thanks to the magic of Chroma-key), perform a few highly visual magic tricks, and then vanish until the next show.

My early television experience taught me a lot about the demand in the marketplace for constant creativity, artistic integrity, and subject matter expertise.

After performing at magic conventions with future headliners like fellow magicians Arsenio Hall and Lance

Burton, I decided to enter the annual competition to crown the top magician, held in Colon, Michigan. My mentor Bill Brewe and I crafted an award-winning magic act that allowed me to take home the top prize in the competition that year!

As a youngster, I was an avid reader of *Boys' Life,* the official magazine of the Boy Scouts of America. Monthly, I raced to my mailbox to get the latest issue of the magazine.

One month I opened the mailbox door, peeked inside— and there he was on the cover of *Boys' Life* magazine. It was me! The cover read, "The Magic Explosion" and featured a photo of yours truly pulling one of my flapping-winged doves from a flowing silk scarf. The accompanying story gave readers a behind-the-scenes look at the annual Abbott's magic contest and the journey to the competition for amateurs, as well as a number of full-time, professional magicians.

That was officially the beginning of my professional magic career. Magic was a great diversion for me in my youth. It kept me out of trouble, and it even paid my way through college. After college, I performed magic for a living on the *Love Boat* and many other luxury cruise liners around the world. Little did I know that one day my magical life would help me educate others about the trickery behind identity theft and fraud.

Today, over thirty years after first discovering the art of performance magic, I incorporate magical vignettes and thought-provoking illusions into my professional presentations and seminars. I use magic to capture the audience's attention and punctuate my speaking points—there's nothing like a clever magic trick to drive home a memorable point.

In 2008, I took my bag of tricks on the road to Asia to perform for locals and tourists alike during the Games of the XXIX Olympiad in Beijing, China.

I prepared not only traditional Western illusions, but a few enchanting effects made famous by a long line of world-class Asian conjurers. By performing these magical effects, I bring my audiences to another level of awareness and, hopefully, enjoyment.

In 2009 I was invited back to China. Again, my gracious hosts were eager to exchange culture, art, cuisine (and English lessons). This time I packed a full stage show, complete with card manipulations, rope tricks, a floating silver sphere, silk-scarf productions, and the centuries-old Chinese linking rings trick.

A Circle of Magical Friends

My longtime friend, corporate consultant, and rainmaker Joel Bauer, refers to theatrically inspired training demonstrations as "transformation mechanisms." These "mechanisms" help to convey and illustrate potentially complex gambits, ruses, schemes, and vulnerabilities in a simple, visual, and memorable way.

Over the past few years, I've learned that professional magicians and identity thieves have quite a few traits in common. This understanding only strengthens my resolve to fight against identity theft.

The differences between the deceptions practiced by the honest magician and the dishonest identity thief are obvious. Both of these deceivers do it for the money.

Their intentions for their "victims," however, couldn't be further apart. One deceiver is purely *theatrical*, while the other is simply *diabolical*.

- Both practitioners are often invited into your space (home or business).
- Both have practiced privately before venturing out publicly.
- Both require a certain amount of trust for their gambits to be effective.
- Both only share secrets of the trade with others of their kind.
- Both have much vested in going undetected for as long as possible.
- Both utilize a form of misdirection to divert your attention and increase your vulnerability.
- Both intend to thoroughly deceive and usually succeed.

Winning Strategies

Through the somewhat unusual combination of my insurance and risk management background, my experience as a professional magician, and my personal struggle with fraud, I like to think that I offer a unique perspective on identity theft. I aim to share some of these perspectives with you in the following chapters.

In the eyes of identity thieves, we're all targets. Although we may not realize it, each of us has arrows coming at us on many fronts at any given moment. Throughout this book, you will learn how to make yourself a smaller target, which will minimize your exposure and decrease your risk of succumbing to an identity theft bull's-eye.

Much like chess, avoiding identity theft is a game of strategy. You have to be able to predict your opponent's next move in order to defeat him. Your goal is to become as savvy about identity theft as you possibly can.

My goal is to share with you not one strategic move, but many.

After all, there is no single cause or cure for identity theft. However, if you employ just one or two strategies from this book, you'll make enormous strides in protecting yourself, your personal identifying information, your loved ones, and your business assets.

Chapter 1
A Rampant Crime: The Disturbing Statistics

For five immature years, I lived a life of illusion and tricks.
—Frank W. Abagnale,
author of *Catch Me If You Can*

How it all Began

According to the Federal Trade Commission, identity theft is "when someone appropriates your personal information (like your social security number or credit card account number) to commit fraud or theft."

Many people assume that identity theft emerged with the dawning of the Internet—but this insidious crime has been around for decades, possibly centuries. Fraudsters have stolen identities, staged elaborate cons, and swindled unsuspecting victims since the beginning of time.

Obviously, the game has changed over the years.

Hundreds of years ago, identity theft was a much grislier crime. What made it so ghastly? The identity thief often had to murder a victim in order to take over his identity.

In days gone by, stealing an identity involved massive amounts of scheming, dramatic disguises, and the threat of severe punishment for the thieves caught in the fraudulent act. Because identity theft was such a complex crime to commit, it was relatively uncommon.

But things have changed. These days, identity theft rarely involves murder or any physical harm at all, for that matter. As a matter of fact, the modern identity thief never even has to come into contact with you to steal your identity. All he needs are just a couple of personal details about you. Lucky for him, this information is readily available in a mailbox, a dumpster, or online. More often than not, the victim doesn't even know that he or she has been hit.

"In the age of instant credit and preapproved credit offers, identity thieves require little more than your name and social security number, plus your date of birth if they get lucky, to assume your identity," Mari J. Frank, Esq. writes in her book *Safeguard Your Identity: Protect Yourself with a Personal Privacy Audit.*

In 2010, Mari also authored *The Complete Idiot's Guide to Recovering from Identity Theft.* A respected leader in the fight against identity theft, Mari Frank is an author, identity theft advocate, attorney, and California State University professor. In *Safeguard Your Identity,* she wrote, "These fraudsters are skillful at using a variety of low-tech *and* high-tech methods to obtain your personal identity."

In other words, identity theft is a much easier crime to commit in modern times. So easy, in fact, that a teenager could pull it off. Take Frank W. Abagnale, for example. He famously practiced the art of identity theft back in the 1960s—when he was only sixteen years old.

Abagnale's Infamous Tale

Unless you were living under a rock in 2002, you probably saw or at least heard about the Oscar-nominated movie *Catch Me If You Can,* starring Leonardo DiCaprio. Based on the autobiographical book of the same title, this wildly popular film follows the fascinating life of a young but internationally renowned con artist.

If you missed out on the book and the movie, here's how this captivating tale goes: At the age of sixteen, Frank Abagnale ran away from home and jumped headfirst into a magical web of lies, cons, and thievery. He quickly became a world-famous imposter and check fraud artist who was sought after by law enforcement officers across the globe.

"I had enjoyed a misguided and regrettable run as one of the most successful con artists the world has ever known," he writes in his second book, *The Art of the Steal.* Here was a kid who had not even made it past the tenth grade, but he successfully posed as a Pan Am pilot, a stock broker, an assistant district attorney, a sociology professor, and even a pediatrician.

But it was the check fraud that eventually put the

con man behind bars. "Through my various hustles, I passed something like $2.5 million worth of checks," he says. "I was proficient enough at cashing fraudulent checks that I earned the distinction of becoming one of the most hunted criminals by the FBI."

Luckily, after serving his time, the criminal switched sides. As a "white-collar crime specialist," he began speaking to banks, businesses, and law enforcement agencies about check fraud. Now regarded as one of the leading experts on counterfeiting and secure documents, he has taught at the FBI Academy and lectures audiences throughout the world.

"In a certain sense, I'm still a con artist," he writes. "I'm just putting down a positive con these days, as opposed to the negative con I used in the past. I've applied the same relentless attention to working on stopping fraud that I once applied to perpetuating fraud."

Identity Theft Reaches All-Time Highs

Although fraudsters, con artists, and hustlers have always been around, identity theft only surfaced as a widespread problem in the mid-1990s. The media first started throwing around the phrase "identity theft" in 1996, when financial crimes against consumers reached an all-time high.

At the time, financial crimes, including loan, mortgage, and credit card fraud, were becoming commonplace throughout the nation—affecting thousands of un-suspecting consumers. Identity theft has continued to grow, spreading like a financial wildfire and taking its victims by surprise.

A Raging Epidemic

"For five immature years, I lived a life of illusion and tricks," Abagnale writes. And that's exactly what these perpetrators do—they put on a flashy little magic show and hide behind a series of diversions to throw victims and law enforcement off their tracks. That's why it's so difficult to catch these sharks and extinguish the flames of the identity theft firestorm.

We truly are facing an epidemic here—the magnitude of the nation's identity theft problem is absolutely mind-boggling. It's a train wreck. I know I've said it before, but it's worth pointing out again: identity theft is the fastest-growing crime in the United States.

But don't take my word for it. Just look at the ever-climbing statistics on this pervasive crime.

Growing, Growing, Still Not Gone ...

In response to the mounting number of consumer fraud and identity theft cases, the Federal Trade Commission set up an online fraud-fighting database called Consumer Sentinel in 1997. The FTC encourages consumers to report fraud and identity theft complaints to this database.

Hundreds of law enforcement agencies throughout the world have access to Consumer Sentinel, which allows them to investigate fraud on a massive scale. The database also helps the FTC keep track of the number of consumers affected by identity theft.

The ever-growing number of complaints reported

to Consumer Sentinel each year is absolutely mind-blowing.

- In 2001, the FTC received 204,000 complaints from consumers saying that they had been the victims of fraud. The number one type of fraud reported was identity theft, representing 42 percent of the complaints.

- In 2002, fraud complaints nearly doubled to 403,688. Identity theft was number one again at 40 percent.

- In 2003, fraud reports jumped to 542,378. No surprise, identity theft topped the list again at 40 percent.

- In 2004, the FTC received 635,591 fraud complaints—triple the number of complaints from just three years before. Of these reports, 38 percent involved identity theft.

- In 2005, fraud complaints reached an all-time high of 693,519. Of those, 37 percent were identity theft reports.

- In 2006, there were 674,354 fraud complaints. Identity theft topped the list for the **seventh year in a row** at 36 percent.

- In 2007, the FTC testified before Congress, stating that stepped-up authentication techniques were needed to protect the social security numbers of over 300 million Americans.

- In 2008, the FTC announced the results of a roundtable attended by experts from government, business, technology, and consumer advocacy groups, as well as academic circles. The roundtable identified a broad range of strategies to immediately educate the public regarding the latest financial self-defense strategies.

- In 2009, the FTC published guidelines for a new Breach Notification Rule requiring the protection of electronic health records.
- In 2010, the FTC will complete a commissioned identity theft study by year's end.[1]

More Eye-Openers

If you're still not convinced that identity theft is growing out of control, here are some more shocking statistics. While each research group uses a different strategy in calculating identity theft, the numbers are astounding any way you look at them.

- Fifteen million people were victims of identity theft in 2006, according to a Gartner Research study. One person falls victim to identity theft every two seconds—that's thirty people every minute!
- In 2006, the total of consumer losses from identity theft was estimated at $1.1 billion, and the median consumer loss was $500 per consumer, according to the FTC.
- Seventy-three million people reported their IDs as lost or stolen in 2006, according to the President's Identity Theft Task Force. Most

1   FTC, *FTC Will Study Experiences of Identity Theft Victims*, Federal Trade Commission http://www.ftc.gov/opa/2008/07 /fcra.shtm (Dec. 9, 2010).

likely, many more IDs were stolen and not reported. Although not all of these incidents led to identity theft, this is a relevant number.

- A whopping 8.4 million US adults were victims of identity fraud in 2007, losing an average of $6,000 each, according to Javelin Strategy & Research.

- In 2007, US consumers and businesses lost $49.3 billion to fraud, according to Javelin Strategy & Research.

- By August 2008, thirty-nine states and the District of Columbia had passed "credit freeze" laws granting consumers the right to protect their credit profile by freezing or thawing access to their credit report on demand. (See full state-by-state **credit-freeze** references at the end of this book.)

- In 2009, a class action suit was filed in US District Court against Heartland Payment Systems for the way it handled what the *Washington Post* has called possibly the largest data breach in history.

- In 2010, hacker Albert Gonzalez was sentenced to twenty years in prison for masterminding the largest data breach in the history of the United States. This breach resulted in the theft of an estimated 130 million credit and debit card numbers. Gonzalez and his coconspirators used a relatively simple technique known as "SQL injection" to penetrate the firewalls of several major retailers, including Heartland Payment Systems, T.J.Maxx, and 7-Eleven, Inc. Over $1 million in cash was recovered from a stash buried in the backyard of Mr. Gonzalez's parents' home in Miami, Florida.

- In 2011, the influential website mashable.com reported that the worldwide cost of identity theft adds up to over $200 billion per year!

- Also in 2011, the growth of cloud-computing, the WikiLeaks saga and the enormous breaches at Epsilon and Sony have raised governmental, corporate, and personal data privacy concerns to alarming new levels.

What's even more disturbing is that these statistics only scratch the surface. FTC fraud complaints and identity theft statistics represent only a fraction of the actual number of victims. Why? It is because many victims simply don't come forward and report the crime, while others haven't discovered that they have been "hit" yet.

Stepping Forward to Move Ahead

According to the FTC, as few as 26 percent of identity theft victims actually report their victimization to police. That means that 74 percent of identity theft victims never reported the crime committed against them. Regrettably, I was one of those silent victims.

When I became a victim of identity theft, I didn't go to the police. I figured that the LAPD was too busy. After all, they're dealing with much more important and high-profile problems than my insignificant identity theft issue. I thought it just wasn't worth bothering them. How wrong I was.

As any law enforcement or forensics expert will tell you,

all criminals leave a signature—no matter how careful or crafty they may be. When victims come forward and report an incident, they increase the likelihood that investigators will pinpoint that criminal's signature and catch the thief—taking him (or her) off the street.

Here's the thing: if law enforcement gets just one identity thief off the street, they've solved not only one mystery, but also possibly multiple mysteries. You see, identity thieves are habitual criminals.

I lectured recently for the National Crime Prevention Council's annual conference. Afterward, an attending undercover police officer succinctly reinforced the importance of victims coming forward. "If victims came forward, we could stop more bad guys in their tracks." Additionally, law enforcement agencies are often hampered by a lack of resources, which makes it more challenging to investigate, identify, and prosecute habitual offenders.

Perpetrators rarely strike just once after they realize how easy it is to get away with a scam. So, if they've stolen your identity, I can almost guarantee that they've stolen countless others, and they're planning to steal more.

If you become a victim of identity theft, I strongly encourage you to report the crime to the police. I sincerely regret that I did not report it myself. By not stepping forward, I probably made my ordeal last much longer than necessary. Had I gone to the police, my struggle may have been a little easier.

Identity theft is not only the fastest-growing crime—it's also one of the most under-prosecuted crimes. That's *not* because these crimes are poorly investigated by law enforcement, but because too many victims are standing in the shadows. Identity theft and fraud are simultaneously the fastest-growing *and* the most underreported crimes in the country. This is a surefire recipe for copycat replication and financial heartburn for victims.

If you become one of the millions of identity theft victims, I urge you to step out of the shadows and report the crime promptly to local law enforcement. Not only could it help you resolve your personal ordeal more quickly, but it may spare others from facing the same nightmare in the future.

Technology: Feeding the Identity Theft Machine?

Many people blame the Internet and technology for the nation's identity theft crisis. "Technology breeds crime and it always has," Abagnale writes in *The Art of the Steal*. "Today, sitting at home in an apartment with a PC, a scanner, a color printer, and a color copier, you can reproduce just about any type of document, including hard cash."

There's no doubt that technology fans the flames of identity theft. As our society continues to introduce innovative new technologies, consumers seem to make more transactions online rather than in person. Consequently, many consumers have become somewhat faceless. This makes a fraudster's job that much easier.

While a great deal of identity theft occurs through Internet schemes, some statistics show that the majority of identity theft still takes place in the real world. A recent study by the Better Business Bureau revealed that online theft accounted for only 12 percent of identity theft cases.

"We still find that most information is stolen in the real world, but it's used extensively in the virtual world of the Internet," Mari Frank says.

In other words, while a great deal of information is stolen the "old-fashioned" way—from wallets, dumpsters, and mailboxes—many identity thieves turn around and use this information online, making unauthorized purchases or setting up fraudulent accounts. Some fraudsters even buy and sell stolen identities in online chat rooms, trading people's names, addresses, and social security numbers in exchange for a few dollars.

It comes down to this: your identity can be stolen anywhere. It can be stolen online or offline, on the World Wide Web or in the real wide world. Identity theft can happen to anyone, anywhere, anytime. We are *all* vulnerable.

You Are a Target—Yes, I'm Talking to You!

In the game of identity theft, nearly every single one of us is a target. According to Sid Kirchheimer, author of *Scam-Proof Your Life* and AARP's *Scam Alert* expert, "Those at risk include pretty much anyone with a bank account or social security card; anyone currently holding or eligible for a credit card or driver's license; and anyone who rents or owns a home." Do you fall into one or all of those categories? If so, you are vulnerable to identity theft.

But here's another puzzling problem: While we are all susceptible to identity theft, it seems that at least half of us don't know how to defend ourselves against it. According to a survey by Harris Interactive, 50 percent of consumers say that they don't know enough to protect themselves from identity theft.

Are you one of those consumers? Do you know how to protect your identity? Are you capable of shielding yourself and your family from the flaming arrows coming at you from all sides?

We may all be targets, but we can make ourselves smaller targets. It *is* possible to outsmart these crafty identity thieves. It all comes down to learning and implementing a few tricks of your own.

Put a Few Tricks Up Your Sleeve

The key to protecting yourself requires at least a little understanding of how identity thieves think and work. You have to get inside their minds and predict their next move—and stay one step ahead of them at all times.

In the following chapters, I'll share some techniques and tips to help you protect yourself and your family. I may be a magician, but unfortunately, I can't make this identity theft problem disappear. What I can do is teach you a few tricks of your own so that you can beat the identity thieves at their own game.

Whatever you do, don't sit back and do nothing. Because, if you drop your guard for one second, *poof!*—your identity is gone. And before you know it, you and your family will be cast in an unforgiving shadow.

Legendary illusionist Harry Blackstone Sr. caused a woman to float effortlessly through the air during every stage performance. At the climax of the illusion, *poof!*—the floating lady literally floated out over the first few rows of the audience and was reported by eyewitnesses to have "vanished like a fading cloud." Don't let Blackstone's disappearing act happen to your good name.

Chapter 1 in a Nutshell

- In today's world of portable data, high-speed networks, and Internet anonymity, identity theft is much easier to commit than it was in the past.

- Identity theft is the fastest-growing crime in the United States. The number of identity theft victims climbs higher every single year.

- Identity theft is also the most under-prosecuted crime. If you become a victim of identity theft, you should report it immediately. By reporting the crime, you can help remove an identity thief from the streets and prevent countless others from suffering the same fate.

- Your identity can be stolen anywhere—both online and in the real world. Although Internet schemes account for a large number of identity theft cases, statistics show that the majority of identity theft still takes place in the real world. This includes information stolen from dumpsters, wallets, and mailboxes.

- No one is immune to identity theft—we are *all* targets. However, you can make yourself a smaller target by following the techniques throughout the following chapters.

- The realities of the twenty-first-century economy have driven many desperate people to foolishly commit financial crimes in a struggle for economic survival.

Chapter 2
Falling Into the Shadows of Identity Theft

Character is like a tree and reputation like its shadow. The shadow is what we think of it; the tree is the real thing.
—Abraham Lincoln

In the last chapter, I presented many compelling figures proving that identity theft has become a national disaster. But there's so much more to this critical crisis. Beneath the surface, there's another thread to the story that the numbers don't reveal.

Hidden behind the statistics are the thousands upon thousands of unfortunate faces—the faces of actual identity theft victims. These millions of victims are people just like you and me. They are your friends, your employees, your neighbors, your colleagues, and your loved ones. Like my situation, one of those faces could even be your own.

While some of these victims recover quickly and fairly easily from identity theft, others suffer greatly for long periods of time. Some are left struggling for months or even years after their identity is stolen.

The Unseen Consequences

Identity theft victims can suffer from much more than financial hardship—these people often bear emotional, professional, and social scars as a result of their victimization.

When a person is suddenly hurled into the shadows of identity theft, they are often left humiliated, their reputation marred, their financial status destroyed— and in some extremely unfortunate cases, their families and relationships are torn apart.

According to the Identity Theft Resource Center (ITRC), a nonprofit national organization that studies and fights identity theft, all victims face a number of unexpected secondary effects in the aftermath of an identity theft event. Take a look at some of the organization's findings, including:

- **Countless hours lost:** On average, victims spent 330 hours recovering from their identity theft ordeal. These hours were often spread out over a number of years. The number of hours victims spent trying to resolve their identity theft issues ranged from just three hours to a whopping 5,840 hours.

- **Domino effect:** Even after an identity thief stops using a person's information, many victims continue to pay the price. Some victims report that they faced higher insurance or credit card fees and higher interest rates.

Many also had to fight collection agencies that refused to clear their record. Some victims suffer from these aftereffects for more than ten years after their identity is stolen.

- **Paying the price professionally:** Some victims say that they were unable to find or keep a job as a result of their identity theft ordeal.

- **Family and relationship problems:** More than 40 percent of identity theft victims reported that they were dealing with an increasingly stressed family life. Sadly, 9 percent of victims said that their relationships with their spouses or significant others was "on the rocks" or ended altogether as a result of the crime.

- **Emotional issues:** Experts compare the emotional trauma of identity theft victims to the pain felt by victims of more violent crimes, such as sexual assault and repeated battery. Identity theft victims report that they feel dirty, defiled, ashamed, and embarrassed or undeserving of help.[2]

The Tree and the Shadow

Why are these identity theft victims suffering on so many different levels? Why are they facing financial, social, professional, and emotional issues? It is because these victims have been cast into the shadows.

2 Identity Theft Resource Center, *Identity Theft Resource Center ITRC Fact Sheet 108*, Identity Theft Resource Center http://www.idtheftcenter.org/artman2/publish/v_fact_sheets/ Fact_Sheet_108_Overcoming_The_Emotional_Impact.shtml (Dec. 9, 2010).

President Abraham Lincoln said, "Character is like a tree and reputation like its shadow." Once the shadow of identity theft falls over you and your family, you feel hopeless, helpless, and victimized. It's a dark, lonely place—and the victims often feel ostracized and misjudged.

But Lincoln also said, "The shadow is what we think; the tree is the real thing." That's exactly why we have to protect that tree, guard our reputation, and minimize that shadow. And we have to teach our children, our parents, and the rest of our family to do the same.

I've got a beautiful family. I'm blessed with a gorgeous wife and great kids. I moved to California as a professional magician many years ago, and I never looked back. Karen and I have worked hard to raise our five exceptional children and to build character into each of them. To build character in our kids, we've got to lead by example, because, as you know, they're always watching.

But my children, as well as yours, are vulnerable, and they're being victimized. Case in point: if one of your kids gets a credit card offer at the age of thirteen, what are you supposed to do about that? It happened to my daughter. Why is a thirteen-year-old getting a credit card offer? How did they get her name? Why did it come in the mail? What happens if she (or her identity) falls prey? Suddenly, she's living in the shadow.

Despite the uncertainty of our current economy, I cherish the financial freedom we enjoy in this country. We have a responsibility to protect families, our future generations, and ourselves. It is no longer enough to teach the next generation to be upright and responsible. We must teach them to financially protect both themselves and their reputations.

Dan Rather once quoted one of his mother's favorite lessons. "Strong trees don't grow at ease . . . the stronger the breeze, the stronger the trees."

When your reputation is taken from you, as mine was taken from me, you feel alone. Identity theft victims feel just as victimized as the victims of violent crimes because the specter of the crime keeps coming back. The threat continues. The fear continues. The hopelessness continues—and more often than not, victims find themselves trapped in that shadow.

It's important to remember that the shadow is what we think—the tree is the real thing. Even after you fall into the shadows of identity theft, you *can* come back to the light. I know this firsthand because I personally survived a trip into the shadows.

My Nordstrom Nightmare

My first inkling that something was wrong was when I got a phone call from Nordstrom. It's a great place to shop (especially during one of those twice-yearly sales), but I wasn't expecting to receive this kind of call.

Why was I surprised to get this call? You see, in financial industry lingo, I was what they refer to as "golden nuggets." That's what we label someone with impeccable credit. Because I've worked in the finance business for many years, I understand the value of good credit and the importance of paying my bills on time. I've tried to plant those roots down deep and build a strong foundation to keep my family out of the shadows.

But all that changed with one call from Nordstrom's collections agency. I assumed that they were calling to invite me to a private sale or to offer me some special perk like an exclusive credit card for elite customers. No such luck. The conversation went something like this:

Collector: Mr. Penn?

Me: Yes.

Collector: I'm calling from the collection department. It seems you bounced a check to us.

Me: No, I didn't.

Collector: Yes, you did.

Me: No, I didn't. I've *never* bounced a check.

Collector: Didn't you write a check to Nordstrom for $212.13?

Me: Nope.

Collector: Mr. Penn, you're going to have to come down here and pay immediately.

Me: I've never bounced a check to you. I don't owe you any money.

Collector: Yes, you do. *(Shouting)* Hey, don't you hang up on me! I'll just call right back!

I was absolutely shocked. I wasn't used to that kind of treatment. *Golden nuggets!* I had golden nuggets of credit.

Before I knew it, multiple collectors began harassing me with aggressive demands like "Hey, don't hang up on me, I'll just call right back! Why did you bounce that check?"

Home Depot called, Walgreens called, PetSmart, and JC Penney. I had so many incoming collections missiles that I didn't know how to stop all that negative momentum. My problem had grown unmanageable and began to develop a life of its own.

My family had been living a relatively modest and comfortable lifestyle for many years. All of a sudden, a shadow was cast over the family. I felt trapped, blindsided, and helpless. Years of building and protecting my financial reputation were jeopardized in an instant.

It happened to me, and it can happen to you. A little research revealed that it even happened to Oprah!

Famously Victimized

As I've mentioned, I live in Los Angeles, lovingly known as La-La Land to some. They say that La-La Land is like a bowl of granola. The ones that aren't seedy or nutty are flaky!

Our family loves the West Coast, and it's no secret that LA is the land of celebrities. It may seem that these "demigods" of the entertainment world would be immune to any kind of financial strife. The truth is that quite a few celebrities have been victims of identity theft.

You would think that it's almost impossible to steal the identity of a high-profile person, but it's not. These fraudsters are amazingly clever. Here are just a few examples:

Oprah: Yes, even Oprah, one of the richest and most famous people in America, has had her identity stolen. She's so well-known that she doesn't even need a last name!

A skilled identity thief targeted Oprah, along with other high-paid executives and celebrities from the Forbes 400 list. He duped credit-reporting agencies into providing detailed credit reports on Oprah, Ted Turner, Steven Spielberg, and many other wealthy Americans from the Forbes list. He used their identities to buy luxurious items and tried to steal nearly $22 million. This proves that *no one* is immune to this pervasive crime.

Tiger Woods: The man who used Tiger's stolen identity to purchase over $17,000 in merchandise was sentenced to 200 years in prison upon conviction under California's 3-strikes law.

***American Idol* winner Ruben Studdard**: How another person masqueraded as Ruben, I don't know. At the height of his media exposure, you would think that it would be a challenge for anyone to impersonate this smooth crooner. Well, I've got news for you; there is a way to impersonate celebrities. It is often somebody close to him or her.

In Ruben's case, it was his personal business manager. The manager stole Ruben's identity and spent more than $250,000 in his name.

That's how a lot of people fall prey to identity theft. Those closest to us—friends, family, and trusted colleagues—often betray that trust and take advantage of their proximity to our valuable assets.

General John M. Shalikashvili: Retired General Shalikashvili, the former chairman of the Joint Chiefs of Staff, has also been a victim of identity theft. How do you impersonate General Shalikashvili? How do you even stroll up to the cash register and pronounce his name? As impossible as it seems, identity thieves pulled it off.

Here's how: Shalikashvili's social security number was published in the congressional record along with the social security numbers of other military officers. That record was then posted on a website. In 1999, fraudsters used the military officers' identities to open 273 new credit card accounts, running up $200,000 in credit card debt.

Herman Munster: He's not even a real person, and yet Herman Munster's identity was stolen and offered for sale . . . well, sort of. CardCops Inc., a Malibu, California, Internet security firm, was monitoring a chat room known for selling stolen credit card numbers and personal information.

During this particular eavesdropping session, CardCops looked on as an oblivious identity thief from outside the United States purchased Herman Munster's identity. The American seller, most likely a fan of *The Munsters*, sold Herman's name, alleged credit card number, address (1313 Mockingbird Lane), and birth date of August 15, 1964—coincidently about when *The Munsters* first premiered on network television.

Unfamiliar with American pop culture, the foreign buyer had no clue that the identity he purchased was that of a fictional character from a popular 1960s TV show. Although somewhat humorous, this story reveals the global scope of this insidious crime.

The Girl Scouts: There's another vulnerable person who lives in my neighborhood and yours: the Girl Scout. While most Girl Scouts may not be considered celebrities, the Girl Scouts of America is nationally recognized as a beloved group for girls.

But in 2007, the Girl Scouts' reputation suffered a serious blow when a troop leader in Pea Ridge, Florida, greatly betrayed the trust of her scouts and their families. Holly Barnes, a mother of four, stole the identities of at least fifteen of her scouts—innocent young girls between the ages of eight and eleven.

Barnes created fraudulent medical release forms to gather the girls' social security numbers and then used their identities to claim more than $87,000 in fraudulent tax refunds from the IRS.

In January 2008, Ms. Barnes was sentenced to ten years in federal prison.

Bonnie and Clyde: In July 2008, Jocelyn Kirsch and Edward Anderton became the most famous couple ever convicted of felony identity theft. The couple netted more than $116,000 in services by stealing the identities of friends and neighbors over a two-year period.

Kirsch and Anderton were dubbed the Bonnie and Clyde of identity theft because of their brazen crimes and the eerie photo journal they maintained as they traveled the world at the expense of their victims.

A federal prosecutor referred to the Philadelphia couple as "the poster children for identity theft."

What Do These Stories Tell Us?

They prove that we are *all* vulnerable. From respected military generals and famous celebrities to innocent Girl Scouts and even fictional characters, we are *all* high-value targets.

Personal data can so easily be taken from us. Our identities are up for grabs in the real world, and they are products, which are easily and routinely bought and sold online. Believe it or not, our information can even be stolen from the businesses and companies we patronize and trust.

Breaches are Bad for Business

Another high profile victim, Federal Reserve Chairman Ben Bernanke, knows first-hand that financial crime is bad for business.

Identity thieves don't always target just one individual at a time. Many of these tricksters have figured out a way to gather hundreds—even thousands—of identities at once. How? They do it by simply targeting businesses.

A number of respected, well-known companies have fallen victim to identity theft over the years. When a company's information is breached, an identity thief can gain access to a virtual gold mine of personal data, sometimes including both consumer and employee information.

Here are just a handful of businesses or institutions that have had customer information yanked from their grasp in recent years:

- **ChoicePoint Inc.:** A ring of identity thieves targeted this national provider of identification and credential verification services in 2005. The fraudsters used falsified information to pose as legitimate businesses and subscribe to ChoicePoint's service. As a result, the thieves gained access to an estimated 140,000 personal accounts and used this information to open new fraudulent accounts in some of the victims' names.

- **Wachovia and Bank of America:** In 2005, Wachovia, Bank of America, Commerce Bank, and PNC Bank became the victims of the largest bank security breach in US history. The thieves stole information from 676,000 New Jersey-based accounts from the four banks. Law enforcement discovered that a ring of bank employees sold the customer account information to a middleman posing as a collection agency, who then brokered it to collection agencies and law firms.

- **T.J. Maxx and Marshall's:** In 2006, TJX Companies, the operator of T.J. Maxx and Marshall's discount stores, fell victim to identity theft. Fraudsters hacked into the company's computer systems, gaining access to the debit and credit card numbers of at least 45.7 *million* customers.

- **TD Ameritrade and E-Trade:** In 2006, TD Ameritrade and E-Trade, two popular online stock brokerages, became victims of a massive stock fraud scheme resulting in $22 million in losses. In what's been labeled a "pump-and-dump" scheme, identity thieves in eastern Europe and Asia hacked into the companies' customer accounts and bought shares in little-traded stocks to drive up prices. They then sold their own previously purchased shares for a profit.

- **Monster.com:** In 2007, monsters invaded http://www.monster.com, a popular job search website. In this massive scheme, cyber thieves stole at least 1.3 million job seekers' personal data from the website. This was a multi-staged attack. The thieves then used the stolen personal data to e-mail Monster.com users with legitimate-looking e-mails advertising job-finding services. If the recipient clicked on a tainted web link in the e-mail, the intruders gained access to their PC—where they could steal even more personal data.

- **Harvard University:** In May 2008, it is believed that a web server may have compromised ten thousand sets of information from the school's applicants and graduate students, resulting in the possible exposure of over six thousand social security numbers, as well as hundreds of Harvard ID numbers.

- **Heartland Payment Systems:** In January 2009, the company revealed that some of the one hundred million transactions per month that it processes were possibly exposed by a malicious software attack on their computer network. According to the banking site http://

www.bankinfosecurity.com, over six hundred financial institutions reported the damage to their cardholders from this single breach.

- **CitiGroup:** In February 2010, CitiGroup mailed tax statements to six hundred thousand customers with their social security numbers printed on the outside of the envelope. Oops!

- **Sony PlayStation:** In April 2011, Sony experienced an enormous data breach which may have affected over 77 million customers.

Escape the Bull's-Eye

As you can see, your personal information is available to identity thieves through countless international channels. In essence, we're all sitting ducks.

Secretly, we've always wanted to stump the trickster at his own game. Use the tips and tricks in the next chapter to help protect your reputation and steer you clear of the hazards that possibly wait.

To make sure your goose isn't cooked, I'm going to teach you some defensive techniques and mind-sets in the next few chapters.

Chapter 2 in a Nutshell

- It generally takes a significant amount of time to resolve identity theft cases. Some victims struggle for months or even years after their identity is stolen.

- Identity theft victims don't just suffer financially. They often suffer emotionally, professionally, and socially, as well.

- Identity theft victims feel just as victimized as the victims of violent crimes.

- To stay out of the shadows of identity theft, we must protect our character and reputation. We have a responsibility to teach our children and other family members to do the same.

- *Anyone* can fall victim to identity theft. It happened to me, and it can happen to you.

- Respected military generals, famous celebrities, and fictional characters have become identity theft victims, proving that we are all vulnerable to this raging crime.

- Identity thieves also target businesses, gaining access to the personal information of thousands of consumers and employees.

- Large corporate and government servers are often targeted by hackers using a DDoS or Distributed Denial of Service attack to paralyze the target organization.

Chapter 3
Tricks for Making Yourself a Smaller Target

Happiness is composed of misfortunes avoided.
—Alphonse Karr

I like to describe the solitude of safety from identity theft as an oasis in the desolate sands of the fraud landscape. In order to gain safe passage to this identity oasis, you have to become proactive.

In other words, you have to start fighting this crime *before* you become a victim, or you may never find the shade and solitude of protection that you, your business, or loved ones seek and deserve.

In earlier chapters, I've pointed out that we are *all* targets for identity theft. With flaming arrows whizzing all around us, it's just a matter of time before you or someone you love gets struck. Luckily, there are some fairly simple steps that you can take to greatly decrease the odds of taking a direct hit.

I've woven my way through the labyrinth of identity

theft for the past few years, trying to learn as much as possible about it. Along the way, I've picked up a lot of proven, effective strategies for avoiding identity theft. My goal is to teach people how to avoid becoming a victim—how to minimize their risks and reduce their chances of facing the nightmare of identity theft.

Be a Shrinking, Moving Target

Marksmen and archery enthusiasts will tell you that the farther away the target, the more difficult it is to hit. And if the target is a moving target, it's even harder to hit. Much like the prey that hunters seek, you must make yourself a smaller target if you want to be less vulnerable to identity theft.

To avoid being hit by identity thieves, you have to become a distant, roving, barely detectable target. The following tricks will help you do just that.

Six Simple Strategies to Avoid Identity Theft

1. **Shred, shred, shred.**

Frank Abagnale said, "One person's trash is another person's treasure!" We have to put a high value on our personal information, including our trash. Identity thieves are not above "dumpster diving," or digging through your trash to find a gem among the garbage. If you toss out just one credit card offer, one bill, one check, or one tax document that includes your personal information, you have made yourself vulnerable.

Consequently, *shredders are not optional*. In your business and in your home, a shredder is *absolutely necessary* for your protection. Tearing up personal documents is not enough. Determined fraudsters will take the time to dig through your trash, recover every last piece of the document, and tape it back together so that they can read and steal your personal data. A crosscut shredder makes this virtually impossible.

So what should you shred? Any document that reveals your valuable personal information, including your name, your address and phone number, your social security number, your account numbers, or any combination of these items.

Here are a few examples of documents you should shred:

- **Bank statements and transaction slips:** You may want to hang onto to your deposit and withdrawal slips until you receive your bank statement each month, but keep these in a safe, secure place—not in your wallet! Once you receive your monthly statement, shred those slips.

- **Loan statements:** Shred your loan documents after you've paid off the sum of your loan.

- **CD records:** After your CD accounts mature and you collect the interest, it's time shred the records.

- **Credit card bills and receipts:** You may want to hang onto credit card bills and receipts for a year in case you need to make a return. But after the year is up, shred those documents. In the interim, keep them in a safe place.

- **Credit card and checking account offers:** Shred these unsolicited mail offers as soon as you receive them unless you plan to apply. Scammers can apply for fraudulent accounts in your name using these offers. Watch your bills for early warning signs of fraud.

- **Investment documents:** Shred your monthly or quarterly investment statements as soon as the new statement arrives.

In case the IRS audits you, some experts recommend that you keep your monthly bank or credit statements for up to seven years (especially if they support tax deductions). If you choose to hang onto any of these personal documents, safely file them away *under lock and key.* Once the documents are seven years old, start shredding.

2. **Scan your credit report three times a year.**

Under the federal Fair and Accurate Credit Transactions Act of 2003 (FACTA), each of the three major credit bureaus (Equifax, Experian, and TransUnion) are required to provide you with a *free* copy of your credit report once every twelve months. However, the credit reporting agencies don't have to send your report until you request it—so you have to make the effort to ask for a copy. Luckily, it's an incredibly easy process.

Just go to http://www.annualcreditreport.com to request your free credit report. You can ask to receive all three credit reports at the same time, or you can request one report at a time. I recommend staggering the credit reports every four months to keep yourself informed throughout the year.

For example, you could request your free report from Equifax in January, from Experian in May, and from

TransUnion in September. This way, you're able to check out your credit report three times a year for free!

I didn't know about this prior to my own ordeal, but I'm doing it now. I was amazed to see how detailed these reports are. My own report delivered about thirty pages of detailed, valuable data about my favorite person . . . *me*.

What Are the Warning Signs?

Your credit report includes important information about your financial history, including your credit card accounts and payment history, car loan and mortgage information, where you have applied for credit, and requests from companies to look at your credit report.

As you scan through your credit report, you should be looking for any inaccuracies, suspicious activity, or new lines of credit that you did not request. If you find errors or discrepancies, this should set off some serious warning bells. Report any unauthorized credit activity immediately to the credit bureaus.

If there are errors, make sure you immediately write to the creditor to have the questionable items corrected or removed. It is okay to write to the companies via e-mail, but ask them to send you a confirmation of receipt and follow-up with a copy back to you in the mail for your records.

3. **Opt out of junk mail.**
Call 1-888-5OPTOUT (or 1-888-567-8688) to stop receiving unsolicited mail, including credit card and insurance offers. Every offer you receive in the mail

puts you at risk for identity theft. Fraudsters can easily steal these offers directly from your mailbox or trash and apply for fraudulent accounts in your name.

"Each year, more than three million Americans discover that credit card accounts have been falsely opened in their name; of these, at least 400,000 can blame the crime on stolen mail," Kirchheimer writes in *Scam-Proof Your Life.*

Why do you receive this mail in the first place? It's because the credit bureaus can legally sell credit information. The direct mail and credit card companies that purchase this information turn around and send you offers based on your demographics and credit payment history. Once you call the opt-out number, this unsolicited mail should stop.

When you call, a representative will ask for your current address, any former addresses you may have had within the past two years, and your social security number. This is one of the few instances when it's okay to give your social security number to someone over the phone.

The reason my kids were receiving junk mail, including the credit card offers for my thirteen-year-old, was because I hadn't opted out. You better believe I've opted out now. If you haven't called this number and opted out yet, do it *today.*

4. **Safeguard and stagger your PINs, passwords, and personal information.**
I cannot stress how important it is to *really* safeguard all of your PINs, passwords, and personal information. Store this information in a safe in your home, keep it

locked up in drawers, or secure it in other places that are out of reach.

Whatever you do, don't leave this information sitting out for the world to see—tacked to a bulletin board in your office, stuck to your fridge with a magnet, or even sitting out on your bedroom dresser. Why? It is because most identity thieves are people you know and trust—people whom you willingly invite into your home. (Read more on this disturbing fact in chapter 6.)

Not only should you safeguard your passwords, but you should also stagger them. What do I mean by "stagger"? Change up your passwords every now and then, and use different passwords for different accounts. Unfortunately, your mother's maiden name is no longer a secret to a capable ID thief.

Your passwords should be cryptic, complicated, and unpredictable. If your beloved cat's name is Fluffy, don't make "Fluffy" the password to all of your accounts, for crying out loud! This is way too obvious. Anyone who knows you and your dear Fluffy could easily guess this password.

"Don't use anything that can be easily guessed by neighbors, coworkers, or strangers who could get their hands on your wallet—a nickname, child's name, pet's name, or your favorite sports team or hobby," Kirchheimer writes. Instead, he suggests that you mix capital and lowercase letters along with symbols and numbers. Or you could combine parts of two unusual words to create one very bizarre password, such as "gastrocumulus" or "cytoplasticity."

You could also combine a foreign word and English word to create an obscure password. The goal is to choose something extremely difficult and virtually impossible to guess. The stranger and longer and weirder your password is, the better.

5. **Surf and scuba safely.**

After my college years, I was a full-time professional magician working on luxury cruise ships all over the world, including the *Love Boat* of television fame. I couldn't wait to get to the Caribbean and learn how to scuba dive.

When I finally joined a scuba-diving class in the Virgin Islands, I wanted so badly to get in the water, but our skilled instructor wouldn't allow it. Instead, we spent the entire first day learning the ten ways *not* to kill yourself.

Beginning dive classes are all about how not to kill yourself. Just like with scuba diving, you've got to learn how to surf the web safely before "getting in the water." Otherwise, you're eventually doomed.

This is why it is vital to establish a mind-set to surf the web safely. Like Dorothy's adventures in Oz, there are countless dangers lurking down the digitally paved roads of the Internet—spyware, malware, and bots (oh my!). We have to keep up our guard every time we log on. We should strive to make ourselves a smaller target and avoid being hit.

Here are the basics of web safety. If you do nothing else to protect yourself online, at least do these things:

- **Install a firewall.** If you have an Internet connection, especially a high-speed connection, you must have a firewall—no ifs, ands, or buts about it. A firewall keeps the intruders and fraudsters out. It protects you and the information you give online, such as passwords, accounts numbers, personal data, etc. Luckily, most new computers come with a built-in firewall. If you have an older computer that doesn't include a firewall, buy and install one as soon as possible. Two trusted and popular third-party providers are Check Point and ZoneAlarm.

- **Use antiphishing toolbars.** In a "phishing" scheme, fraudsters send out bulk e-mails that lure the recipients to click on a link. This link then leads the unsuspecting victim to a legitimate-looking website, where they are often prompted to give user information, passwords, and account numbers.

For example, you may receive an e-mail that appears to be from eBay asking you to click on a link and update your personal information. If you click on the link, it leads you to a fake website that looks practically identical to eBay's real website. When you enter your personal data onto one of these fake sites, it falls into the hands of identity thieves. These criminals then turn around and open fraudulent accounts or make purchases in your name.

"Phishing attempts are such dead-on mimics—hard for even Internet security experts to detect—that scrutinizing the web address itself may be the best way to spot them," Kirchheimer says. Oftentimes, these fake web addresses are just one letter off from the legitimate site. For example, instead of "http://www. dalepenn.com," the fake address may be "http://www.

dalepen.com," which contains just one less *n* than my legitimate website address.

Antiphishing toolbars (Mozilla offers one of several antiphishing software programs currently available in today's marketplace) are prevalent and plentiful and can help you avoid these phony websites altogether. These toolbars can alert you when you have stumbled upon one of these "phishing" sites.

More importantly, you should just assume that e-mails requesting personal information "updates" are scams. Your credit card company or bank will never ask you to update your account online or over the phone. If you do have an online account with a company and receive an e-mail asking you to update your information, do not click on the link in the e-mail. Instead, go online and type in the actual web address. More than likely, you'll log onto your secure account and discover that no updates are needed after all—which confirms that the e-mail you received was bogus.

- **Use antivirus, antispam, and antispyware software.** There's a great variety of online protection software out there. Buy it and use it. You can install antivirus and antispyware programs to scan your computer weekly or even daily to ensure that you have not been infected. Antispam products alert you when you receive what may be phony, suspicious, or virus-infected e-mails. All of these products are worth their weight in gold, and they are absolutely essential for every Internet-connected computer.

- **Regularly update protection software.** When you install your antispam, antivirus, and antispyware software, choose the option to be notified of any software updates as they become available. Whenever the software notifies you that an update is available, click on the "install" or "update" button. This ensures that you have the latest and greatest protection tools for your computer. Automatic updates that run while you sleep are even better!

Teach your family members and anyone else who uses your computer to do the same. Make sure that they know to always accept updates from your online protection software. This is an easy way to help make you and your family a smaller target.

- **Consider an alternative browser.** As the most popular Internet browser, Microsoft's Internet Explorer comes preinstalled on most new computers. But Microsoft products are also the most frequently attacked. Why? It is because fraudsters know that Microsoft is the most widely used software, so they target those products with their viruses, spyware, and other scams. Even if you are a Mac user, don't drop your guard.

  You should think about switching to a lesser-known browser. There are several Internet browsers out there (Google's Chrome, for example) that are a little less likely to be attacked by maliciously coded software, also known as "malware." Two additional browsers that come highly recommended are Firefox and Opera. You can download these browsers for free at http://www.getfirefox.com or http://www.opera.com.

6. **Build a step-by-step resolution plan.**

I developed a step-by-step resolution plan for my commercial clients. If one of my clients becomes the victim of fraud, this plan does four things for them:

- It gives them education, awareness, and prevention information.

- It gives them restoration, an 800 number to call, and a personal identity theft advocate to help walk them through the entire recovery process.

- It provides compensation for those benefits that are covered under the terms of the plan, which is insured by a top-rated carrier.

- It provides ongoing observation and credit monitoring with instant e-mail and SMS text cell phone alerts in the event of an incident.

That's what I provide my clients—but a step-by-step resolution plan doesn't need to cost money. It can begin with following the six protection steps I've outlined throughout this chapter.

Follow These Six Prevention and Resolution Steps:

In the unfortunate event that you do become an identity theft victim, there are some steps you can take to resolve your crisis relatively quickly and easily. You'll learn more about these critical steps in chapter 7, where I present a step-by-step resolution plan for identity theft victims.

In review, these are the six simple steps you should take right now to protect yourself and your family from identity theft:

1. **Buy a crosscut shredder and destroy all personal documents before discarding them.**
2. **Scan your credit report three times a year for free.**
3. **Opt out of junk mail.**
4. **Safeguard and stagger your PINs, passwords, and personal information.**
5. **Surf the web safely.**
6. **Build a step-by-step resolution plan in case of unforeseen incidents.**

If you follow these six simple steps, you'll be well on your way to making yourself a smaller target. See the resource chapter at the back of this book for details on executing these steps.

Remember, shredders are not optional!

I know we've already been over this, but it's worth reiterating. In this day and age, shredders are no longer a luxury or an optional item. Every household, every office, every person should own a shredder—and you should use it religiously.

Rob Cockerham's Lesson: Why Tearing It Up Isn't Enough

Rob Cockerham gave me permission to share his amazing story with you. If this doesn't drive home the fact that shredders are absolutely necessary in today's world, I don't know what does.

Rob is a clever fellow and self-described prankster who runs http://www.cockeyed.com—a unique website that covers everything from how to fight back against spammers to answering the age-old question: "How many stalks of celery can be stuffed into one jar of peanut butter?" (For the record, it's fifty-seven stalks.)

In one particularly enlightening experiment entitled, "The Torn-Up Credit Card Application," Rob illustrates just why everyone needs a shredder. Here's how the story unfolds.

Rob received a preapproved credit card application from Chase Bank. In the past, Rob had always just torn these applications in half and thrown them away. But this time, he decided to do things a little differently. He ripped the application to shreds and then taped the little shredded bits of paper back together again.

After he taped the application back together, Rob decided to fill out the form. Even though it was obvious that the application had been destroyed and then taped back together, he thought he'd give it a shot to see what would happen.

When he filled out the form, he checked the box on the application requesting an address correction. In the space provided, Rob requested that they send the credit card to his dad's address instead of his address.

"I had a few weeks before I would know if my terribly mangled application would be accepted or rejected, so I did some research on the web," Rob writes.

During his research, he came across Chase Bank's website about protecting your identity. The site says that if you receive a credit card offer you don't want, you should just tear it up before throwing it away. "This was bad news," Rob writes. "Maybe my card would never come."

But two weeks later, Rob got a call from his dad, who informed Rob that some mail had arrived for him. And guess what it was? It was his brand-new, shiny Chase MasterCard with a $10,000 limit—sent to another address after he had torn up the application and taped it back together.

I know it seems unreal, but this actually happened. You can check it out for yourself on http://www.cockeyed. com. This proves just how easily an identity thief can go dumpster diving, retrieve a torn-up credit card application, apply for a card in your name—and even have it sent to his own address!

So what's the lesson here? Do I really need to say it again? If you don't already own a shredder, buy a good one today and start using it!

As Rob says on his website, "Perhaps a good solution would be for credit card applications to come packaged with a coupon to buy a new shredder!" Not a bad idea.

Misfortunes Avoided

Alphonse Karr, a renowned philosopher, once said, "Happiness is composed of misfortunes avoided." Believe it or not, he's the same guy that said, "The more things change, the more they stay the same."

As different as these quotes may seem, both of these truisms apply to identity theft. "Happiness is composed of misfortunes avoided." Those who are proactive and take the proper steps to protect themselves will avoid the misfortune of identity theft. And I can tell you firsthand that avoiding this terrible crime is certainly something to be happy about.

Then again, "The more things change, the more they stay the same." No matter how much the world changes, how much new technology is introduced, how many fraud-fighting task forces are formed, identity theft will continue to rage on. That's exactly why we can't let our guard down. No matter how safe or protected we may feel, we must continually strive to make ourselves smaller targets.

Chapter 3 in a Nutshell

- You must be proactive to avoid identity theft. By making a few lifestyle changes now, you can save yourself from a lot of turmoil later.

- To decrease your risk of becoming a victim, make yourself a smaller target. You can do this by following six simple steps:

  1. Buy a shredder and shred all personal documents before discarding them.
  2. Scan your credit report (for free) at least three times a year.
  3. Opt out of junk mail.
  4. Safeguard and stagger your PINs, passwords, and personal information.
  5. Surf the web safely.
  6. Build a step-by-step resolution plan (see chapter 7).

- Rob Cockerham's ingenious experiment proves that tearing up credit card offers is not enough. To protect yourself from identity theft, you *must* buy a crosscut shredder and use it.

Chapter 4
Fighting Back with the Three Ds

*Happy is he who dares courageously
to defend what he loves.*

—Ovid

"Deter. Detect. Defend." The Federal Trade Commission and the National Crime Prevention Council coined this ingeniously simple slogan. Built on the foundation of three clear-cut commands, this short and snappy phrase truly covers the bases we need to explore about how to fight back against identity theft. If you can't remember anything else about identity theft, you should at least commit the "3D" motto to memory.

Deconstructing the Three Ds

"Deter. Detect. Defend." I like to call this catch phrase "the three Ds." Our mission is to deter, detect, and defend ourselves, both personally and professionally.

The FTC really nailed it. It is difficult to improve upon that slogan because of its simplicity and completeness.

Because the three Ds are so vital to our survival in today's fraud-filled world, it's important that we fully understand and absorb these words. So let me break it down even further.

Deter Means to Modify

The word "deter" is a reminder to each of us to modify our behavior—whether it's being more careful with our mail, being cautious about the conversations we have on the phone, or making ourselves aware of what's going on around us when we're at an ATM. It's all about changing our routine behaviors to minimize risk.

According to the FTC's website, "While nothing can guarantee that you won't become a victim of identity theft, you can minimize your risk, and minimize the damage if a problem develops, by making it more difficult for identity thieves to access your personal information."

As I've mentioned before, the best way to fight back against identity theft is to avoid becoming a victim in the first place. And if you want to dodge those identity theft arrows that are coming at you, you have to make yourself a distant, barely detectable target.

"You must continually be proactive," writes Abagnale. "Practiced today by increasingly wily criminals, fraud is incredibly complex and full of nuance and creativity. The most effective strategy to prevent it is to make things difficult and complicated enough to raise a murmur of distress from the crook. That way he'll decide it's not worth the effort to try and take advantage of you."

Don't make yourself an easy target. If you take a few steps to modify your behavior, it will make things a little too difficult for that fraudster who's thinking about nabbing your identity. By making just a few lifestyle changes, you'll greatly minimize your risk of becoming a victim.

"In our increasingly data-saturated society where information can be accessed, retrieved easily, and shipped anywhere in a nanosecond, criminals have a leg up," Mari J. Frank points out in *From Victim to Victor.* "We cannot be responsible for our information that is stolen when it is out of control. This is frustrating, since we have limited power to reduce access to our information in commerce. There are some things you can easily do to protect yourself, actions you can *personally* take to minimize your risk."

It's this simple: If you want to protect yourself and minimize your risk, you have to make yourself a smaller target. If you follow the six steps I presented in the last chapter, you're already on the right path. If you don't follow those steps, you might as well strap a glowing neon sign to your forehead that says, "Steal my identity, please!"

Detect Means to Monitor

We've got to monitor all of our incoming mail and phone calls, our bank statements, our credit card statements, and every piece of information that we receive. Each of these items can give us clues that something may be going awry. By not monitoring our personal information, we are giving up.

If you receive a statement for a credit card account you did not open, don't toss it out. If you get a phone call about a bounced check that you didn't write, don't ignore it. It's easy to assume that such a phone call or piece of mail is just a random mistake—but these things should set off blaring warning sirens in your mind.

Unfortunately, in today's world, we don't always have the luxury to look on the bright side and expect the best. We have to carefully observe all of our personal information and pounce on any tiny piece of information that seems the least bit suspicious.

According to the FTC, these are some other signs that indicate that you may be the victim of identity theft:

- You receive information about accounts you didn't open or find debts on your current accounts that you can't explain.

- You discover fraudulent or inaccurate information on your credit reports, including accounts and personal information, such as your social security number, current or previous address, name or initials, and employers.

- You fail to receive bills or other regularly expected mail. Follow up with creditors if your bills don't arrive on time. A missing bill could mean an identity thief has taken over your account and changed your billing address.

- You receive credit cards even though you didn't apply for them.

- You are denied credit or offered less favorable credit terms—like a higher interest rate—for no apparent reason.

- You receive calls or letters from debt collectors or businesses about merchandise or services you didn't buy.

As I mentioned earlier, one of the most important items we have to monitor is our credit report. Who else is going to call you up and tell you that something out of the ordinary has popped up on your credit report? It is *your* responsibility to order that report, scrutinize it, and report any suspicious activity, unauthorized accounts, or inaccurate items.

So many people do not discover that they've become a target until it's too late and the damage has already been done. Often, identity theft victims don't find out until they're applying for a loan of some sort.

Assuming that their credit history is immaculate, these unsuspecting victims might apply for a car loan or a mortgage. When the loan or credit is denied, they're left confused and astounded. Only then do they discover that there's something inaccurate on their credit report—often an unauthorized account or credit card that is quickly accumulating debt.

This is a terrible way to discover that you've become a victim of identity theft. Be proactive and check your credit report frequently. Don't put it off another day. Go to http://www.annualcreditreport.com to order your report right now.

Your credit report can be quite informative when you look back at your old habits, patterns, and practices. One of the questions you may have is why your data hasn't been compromised already, given the fact that a large number of your old creditors are no longer in business. Where did all of your "dead data" go?

In a recent blog post, I reported on the number of failed businesses that simply abandon their data or thoughtlessly toss it into a dumpster. Mountains of juicy tidbits have been left in the trash for scavengers to consume.

I urge you to review your report at least three times a year. If you check it frequently enough, you'll be able to catch suspicious activity before the fraudster can cause irreversible damage.

Defend Means to Mitigate

Once you discover that you are a victim of identity theft, you can't just throw your hands in the air and surrender. You have to defend yourself! If you do nothing to fight back, your nightmare will only get worse. If you sit back and wait for someone else to resolve the problem, you're going to be waiting for a long time—probably forever.

After my own experience with identity theft, I realized that my ordeal could have been much shorter and less painful had I immediately defended myself. Instead, I chose to keep quiet. I chose not to report the crime. It was a bad choice, and I still regret it.

Now I understand that there are certain things we can do to mitigate the negative effects of identity theft. The moment you believe that you've become a victim, you should *immediately* take the steps to resolve the problem. It can take years for a victim to recover from identity theft—and the longer you wait to report the crime and take the proper resolution steps, the longer it will take you to recover your financial health.

"Take steps to respond to and recover from identity theft *as soon as you suspect it*," the FTC advises. In chapter 7, I will walk you through these critical steps.

I won't lie to you; resolving a case of identity theft is not a simple process. It is also definitely not an enjoyable process either. Resolution is a process that you must walk through if you want to survive the effects of this crime.

The other alternative is to do nothing—an option that can lead to dire consequences. If you do nothing to defend yourself against identity theft, you are basically allowing your credit, your good name, and your financial health records to be tampered with or perhaps destroyed. You are casting yourself and your family into the shadows.

If you get hit with one of those identity theft arrows, don't just give up and wave your white flag. Defend yourself. Mitigate the consequences. Minimize the negative effects. Walk through the appropriate pre-planned steps to end your nightmare.

Three Simple Words—One Profound Meaning

Deter. Detect. Defend. These three simple, yet powerful words truly encompass everything we need to know about fighting back against identity theft. I implore you to sear these three words into your mind, preach them to your friends and loved ones, and incorporate this mantra into your daily routine.

But you can't just talk the talk . . . you've got to walk the walk. If you want to protect yourself from identity theft, you have to incorporate these three tactics into your lifestyle. In the next chapter, I'll show you how you can put these ideas into action simply by looking around your home.

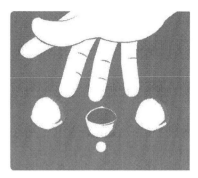

Chapter 4 in a Nutshell

- Modifying your habits and behavior are crucial new habits to maintain.

- Monitoring your credit will be a lifelong pursuit.

- Mitigating the effects of an identity assault is a worthy pursuit.

- Financial and medical records are routinely tossed out when companies go out of business.

- It is prudent to look for telltale signs that your data may have been tampered with.

Chapter 5
Home Improvement:
Shelter Your Home from
Identity Theft

*The strength of a nation is derived
from the integrity of its homes.*
—Confucius

I've already covered simple steps you can take to fight back against identity theft with the three Ds: deter, detect, defend. If you commit this catchy phrase to memory and incorporate these tactics into your life, you will greatly reduce your odds of becoming a victim.

However, I believe that it's absolutely critical that we all fully understand how to protect ourselves against this pervasive crime. I realize that identity theft can be a difficult concept for many people to grasp, especially older generations who are not intimately familiar with the crime.

For that reason, I want to give you another umbrella of identity theft-fighting tactics to consider and perhaps share with the older members of your family. Basically, this simple strategy all comes down to home improvement.

There's No Place Like Home

The majority of us spend a great deal of time at home—after all, home is a sanctuary and a cherished place for most people. It's where we bond with our families, peel back our public façade, and let our true selves shine through. It's a safe haven where we can kick off our shoes and relax. Because we assume we're secure within the confines of our home, it's also where we let down our guard.

The unfortunate reality is that the potential for identity theft follows you even into your own home. You may think that as long as your computer is protected from cyber intruders, your identity is safe within the borders of your house. This is a common misconception.

You see, the majority of identity thieves don't steal your personal data from a computer. According to a Better Business Bureau study, most identity thefts still take place offline, not online. And many of these "real-world" thefts occur in and around the one place where you thought you were safe: your own home.

Under One Roof

I believe that studying and scrutinizing some of the decorative and practical aspects of your home can help families better understand the vulnerability they actually face. I call this the "home improvement strategy." By looking at your home in a new light, you'll be reminded to protect yourself against this insidious crime.

Here are a few common household items you probably encounter on a daily basis. I hope seeing these items will remind and prompt you to protect yourself against common but effective identity theft threats.

Trash can: Your biggest personal information database is right there on the curb every Wednesday morning. Seeing rows upon rows of trash cans lined up and down a suburban street is enough to set a greedy identity thief salivating.

"Identity thieves dumpster dive to fish unshredded loan and credit card applications from the trash of households and businesses," Mari Frank points out in *Safeguard Your Identity: Protect Yourself with a Personal Privacy Audit.*

Some identity-stealing scoundrels don't even have to get their hands soiled in the process. That's because these clever thieves hire someone else to do their dirty work—your trash collector.

"The simplest thing criminals do is to tell garbage collectors that for every intact credit card they find in the garbage and turn over to them, they'll pay them thirty-five dollars," Abagnale writes in *The Art of the Steal.* He points out that even if the card is expired, these tricky thieves will find a way to modify them and put them to work.

"Even though credit card companies repeatedly admonish cardholders to cut up their old cards before discarding them, I'm amazed that most people don't,"

Abagnale says. "They assume that because the card's expired, it's worthless, so just toss it in the trash."

As Rob Cockerham's torn-up credit card application experiment so deftly illustrates, shredding old credit cards is even more effective than cutting them. Here's yet another reason for you to purchase a crosscut shredder right away. A good shredder can obliterate a credit card in seconds.

I can't stress enough how important it is to shred all of your personal information, including credit card applications, bank statements, mortgage statements, and loan applications, before throwing these documents in the trash. Seeing your garbage can at the end of the driveway this week should serve as a reminder to shred, shred, shred.

Front door: Every day as we leave our homes, we go through the front door. Every home has one—at least every home that I've ever seen.

The bulk of identity theft is a result of the people you let into your home—those folks who stroll right through your front door. Who you allow into your home can affect your vulnerability. I'll cover more on this topic in the next chapter, "The Shocking Identities of Identity Thieves."

Windows: Those beautiful windows in your home framed by lovely curtains allow you to look out into the world. Unfortunately, these lovely windows also allow others to look inside. Determined fraudsters are constantly trying to peer into our lives, hoping to glean just enough information to nab our identities.

I'll bet I know what you're thinking. "I've never seen

an identity thief looking through my window." Although it is possible for a thief to steal personal information simply by peeking through a window, I use the window metaphor to serve as a crucial reminder. It's a concept that may help you or your elderly parents remember how vulnerable we all are to this pervasive crime. You never know who may be watching.

While identity thieves may not literally be peeping through your windows, they are catching glimpses of your life through your personal data—readily available in your trash cans, on your computer, and in your mailbox. Your windows should serve as a constant reminder that we are all at risk of becoming victims.

Mailbox: The FTC reported recently that nearly four hundred thousand Americans became victims of identity theft as a result of stolen mail. Long gone are the days when our mailboxes were considered untouchable and safe from the hands of criminals.

Even though stealing mail is a federal crime, identity thieves are willing to take the risk. After all, depending on what they find in your mailbox, the payoff could be huge.

"Thieves steal mail from mailboxes to obtain bank and credit card statements, preapproved credit offers, utility statements, driver's license numbers, social security numbers, and tax information," writes Mari J. Frank. If the thief finds a credit card statement, including your account number or a signed check, he's hit the jackpot.

"Sometimes credit card companies find it convenient to have you write your account number on the outside of your remittance envelope," Abagnale writes.

"Criminals will drive up to your mailbox, look for just those envelopes, and take down your account number. Never write your account number on the outside of an envelope. You might as well take out a newspaper ad advertising your credit to the world."

It is critical to secure your incoming and outgoing mail. As I've mentioned before, you can minimize incoming mail by opting out of unsolicited mail offers. You will see an immediate reduction in your junk mail.

Never leave mail in your mailbox overnight or on weekends. If you're going out of town, ask the post office to hold your mail until you return.

Outgoing mail is another huge risk. Be vigilant about what personal information you leave in your mailbox, and *do not raise the flag* on your mailbox. This lets the fraudsters know that your important PINs, passwords, account numbers, and checks could be waiting for them in the mailbox. This is one red flag that none of us can afford to wave.

Better yet, don't put any mail containing personal information in an unlocked mailbox in the first place. These days, your safest bet is to drop your mail in a locked US Postal Service collection box. It may seem like a hassle, but it's well worth the extra effort.

Telephone: These days, a lot of families are using Voice Over Internet Protocol, or VoIP, instead of regular telephone service. VoIP, which allows you to make phone calls over the web, is becoming increasingly popular throughout the country. Unfortunately, this new technology has also led to yet another identity theft technique: vishing. This scam can affect anyone with a telephone, whether they use VoIP or not.

"Vishing is really just a new take on an old scam—phishing," according to the FBI's website. "First, VoIP service is fairly inexpensive, especially for long distance, making it cheap to make fake calls. Second, because it's web-based, criminals can use software programs to create phony automated customer service lines."

Vishing usually goes down one of two ways. After setting up their fake VoIP customer service line, the thieves either send customers an e-mail asking them to call the phony number, or they call the consumer directly. They then ask the victim to give them account information over the phone to update their account. Oftentimes, these criminals already have some information about the victim's account, which makes the call seem legitimate.

These kinds of scams are very difficult to track and trace. "Criminals can mask the number they are calling from, thwarting caller ID," according to the FBI site. "And in some cases, the VoIP number belongs to a legitimate subscriber whose service is being hacked."

If you receive a call from someone who claims to be with a financial institution, and that person asks for any personal information, hang up. Immediately call the number provided on your credit card or bank statement. That way, you'll know for sure that you are speaking with the actual financial institution as opposed to an imposter.

Computer: Dangers are lurking in every computer, especially those with an Internet connection. Please remember that this includes your smartphone, eBook reader and tablet computing device! As I've mentioned before, we have to learn how to surf the web safely.

Protect yourself and your family from spyware, malware, and viruses by installing firewalls and Internet protection software. (See chapter 3 for a refresher on how to safely surf the web.)

Safe: Do you have a safe in your home where you store valuables or guns? If so, this should be a reminder that you also need to safeguard your personal information.

If you are holding onto any records or documents that include sensitive, personal data, don't just leave them sitting out on a desk or filed away in an unlocked cabinet. To a thief, this information is as valuable as your jewels. Keep personal documents under lock and key, either in a secure safe or a locked file cabinet.

Washing machine: When you walk by your washing machine, it should remind you about playing it safe with your bank checks. Sounds a little odd, doesn't it? Let me explain.

Your washing machine should call to mind a scam known as "check washing." A check washer was the kind of fraudster that got me. Remember my surprise call from Nordstrom, followed by countless other businesses complaining about my bounced checks? It turns out that a check-washing scheme is what led to my identity theft nightmare.

A check-washing scam is surprisingly simple. First, a thief gains access to checks you've written out to anyone like utility or credit card companies. He then uses chemicals found in common household products to "wash the check," erasing everything you wrote in your own hand. The bank's printing—like account information—remains intact.

"All sorts of simple chemicals, like acetone, are used to modify checks," Abagnale reveals in *The Art of the Steal.* The reality is that acetone, most commonly found in nail polish remover, makes anything that's not a "base ink" disappear from a check.

"In a matter of seconds, everything that was put there by a typewriter, laser printer, jet printer, matrix printer, ballpoint pen, or flair pen is off the check," he explains. However, the bank logo, check borders, and check number remain. All the thief needs to add to the washed check is the same fake signature of yours that appears on the homemade driver's license he made earlier with your name on it.

Oftentimes, the fraudster then calls the bank with your account number to find out how much money is in your account. This is how the fraudster knows the size of his catch before pulling the net out of the water.

Luckily, there is a line of defense against check-washing scams, and it's as simple as a two-dollar pen. The type of ink found in gel pens manufactured by the company Uni-Ball is resistant to acetone and other check-washing chemicals. Abagnale personally endorses the Uni-Ball 207 pen, and so do I. I just don't get paid for the endorsement.

So, if you want to write wash-proof checks and protect your bank account, invest in a few of these two-dollar pens. Better yet, don't use checks at all. With the convenience and security of online banking, why are you still using checks? It's not a risk worth taking. I'll cover the advantages of online banking in chapter 8.

Home Sweet Home

After I endured my own identity theft nightmare and learned how to better protect my family, I started wondering, *How do I drill these protection ideas into my parents?* That's why I devised this "home improvement strategy." I thought that it would be a simple way to explain identity theft to my parents and would serve as a powerful reminder for them of how to protect themselves.

This "home improvement strategy" concept really resonates with older generations like my parents. Identity theft is a somewhat complex concept that can be difficult to explain. In days gone by, previous generations didn't have to worry about this crime on a day-to-day basis.

However, it's important to teach everyone in your family how to protect themselves—young people, seniors, and everyone in between. This "home improvement strategy" is the perfect way to do that. Now, every time our parents walk around their home, they will be reminded about how they can avoid identity theft. Hopefully, you will, too.

A Powerful Tool for Financial Health

"An ounce of prevention is worth a pound of cure." We've had these words drilled into us since youth.

I sincerely hope that you will never have to walk through the identity theft resolution steps I present in this book. As a former victim, I know how incredibly cumbersome and emotionally draining it is to claw your way out of the identity theft shadows. I wouldn't wish such a terrible fate on anyone.

But, as I've mentioned before, you can't simply wish and pray that you'll never become a victim of this crime. You can't merely wave your magic wand or enclose your identity in an "invisible cloak" to protect it from these fraudsters.

My long-time friend, Las Vegas comedy magic entertainer Mac King does actually demonstrate the "magical" powers of an invisible cloak in his hilarious award winning act.

The identity theft arrows are constantly whizzing around. It's only a matter of time before we get nailed— unless we take some drastic measures to shield our identities.

I cannot stress enough how important it is to take steps to protect yourself and your family at every turn. I've presented a variety of identity theft protection systems in previous chapters. Hopefully, one of these techniques has hit home with you.

Be on guard, thinking defensively. Use these techniques as weapons to protect yourself and your loved ones. Here is another defensive weapon to add to your toolkit.

Secure Your Identity with Secure MIPC

The website http://www.myfico.com, a division of Fair Isaac Corporation, offers an extremely effective identity theft prevention pneumonic tool called "Secure MIPC." The company reveals this valuable method in their report entitled, "Identity Theft and You."

"The best way to keep criminals from misusing your identity is to prevent them from stealing it in the first place," the myFICO report states. "By following a few simple steps, consumers can dramatically reduce the chances of falling victim to identity theft."

To help consumers better shield their identities, myFICO came up with an easy-to-recall acrostic device. The report reveals an easy way to remember what you need to do to help prevent identity theft. You just need to remember "Secure My PC" and change it to "MIPC." Secure your **m**ail, **i**dentifying information, **p**ayment tools, and your **c**omputer.

Here's how Secure MIPC breaks down:

M = Mail

According to an identity fraud survey report from Javelin Strategy & Research, nearly one in ten identity theft victims who ultimately discovered how their identity was stolen said it happened at the mailbox. As I've mentioned in previous chapters, in this day and age, you *must* secure your incoming and outgoing mail.

Incoming mail should come to a locked box only. If your mailbox is not locked, identity thieves can easily swipe credit card offers and other personal data from it. Purchase a locking mailbox and collect your incoming mail from it as promptly as possible.

You can also minimize incoming mail by opting out of unsolicited mail offers. Once again, simply call 1-888-5OPTOUT (1-888-567-8688) to stop receiving unsolicited mail. When you call, a representative will ask for your current address, former addresses, and your social security number. After you make the call, you will see an immediate reduction in your junk mail.

Outgoing mail is another problem. I used to love to get a little fresh air by strolling down the driveway to put mail in my mailbox. But those days are gone.

There is no good reason to put valuable personal information in your mailbox anymore. If it's just a postcard, that's one thing. But anything with sensitive data or personal information should go only into a locked and protected mailbox. According to myFICO, we should put all outgoing mail in a secure US Postal Service mailbox instead of leaving it in our mailbox at home.

Let's say that you decide to take a risk and put outgoing mail in your own mailbox. Okay, but whatever you do, don't raise that little red flag. It's like a beacon to the identity thieves signaling, "Hey, there's some valuable personal data in here that you may want to check out!"

I = Information

There's a cornucopia of personal identifying information residing within each of our lives and homes. It's so important to protect your personal data—even from those people you think you can trust.

"Remember, the more people who have access to your sensitive personal information, the higher the likelihood of identity theft," the myFICO report states.

It should be clear by now that we to need protect all of our private information, such as PINs, passwords, and account numbers. The granddaddy of them all, of course, is your social security number. When identity thieves get their dirty little paws on a valid social security number, they've hit the jackpot.

Don't ever carry your social security card in your wallet. Keep it in a secure, locked place in your home. Do not provide your social security number to any unknown person or company. You should only provide this information if it is absolutely necessary.

Keep a list of all your account numbers, PINs, and passwords locked away in a safe place. And once again, I can't stress this enough—buy a crosscut shredder and pulverize anything that includes personal data. Do not toss these little treasures in the trash. You might as well dump the contents of your wallet into the garbage.

If you can protect your personal identifying information, you'll go a long way in preventing identity theft.

P = Payment tools

It's vital that you protect any tools (hint: checks and credit or debit cards) you use for making payments. Keep all of these payment tools, as well as their accompanying PINs and passwords, locked away and out of reach.

"Always make sure that all your payment tools, such as credit cards, debit cards, checks, and account information are secure and not easily accessible, even by friends, relatives, and neighbors," the myFICO report advises.

Here are some extra measures you should take to protect each of your payment tools.

1. **Checks:** If you're in the habit of writing account numbers in the memo line of your checks, stop it! If a thief steals the check from your mailbox, he now has your bank information, as well as the account number for the bill you're paying.

   Also, for personal checks, try not to include your full name, address, and phone number on your checks. It's not necessary. An initial that doesn't identify your gender goes a long toward protecting your identity. Simply include your first initial and your last name on your checks.

   Never, ever write or print your social security number on a check. "Don't allow merchants to write it on checks either," Mari J. Frank writes. "Retailers don't need it—thieves do."

   But when it comes right down to it, you should very rarely use checks, if at all. "You are safer using a credit card to buy groceries, gas, products, and services than you are using a check," Frank points out. Plus, with the convenience and security of online banking, there's no longer a need to write checks to pay your bills.

   The media and financial experts seem to go back and forth on whether online banking is safer than "paper banking." But remember—the majority of identity theft occurs outside of the cyber world, not online.

As a matter of fact, people who bank entirely online can reduce their chances of becoming identity theft victims by 10 percent, according to a study by James Van Dyke, President of Javelin Strategy & Research.

If online banking seems uncomfortable to you, speak with your banker about your safety concerns. The world is going paperless, so you may want to jump out ahead of the curve.

Online banking customers also find that it's much easier to monitor their accounts than those who wait to receive their monthly paper statements in the mail. According to another Javelin Strategy & Research study, it took online bankers an average of eighteen days to detect fraud. On the other hand, it took paper users an average of 114 days to discover that their account had been compromised.

As long as your computer is fully defended with firewalls, anti-spyware, anti-virus, and other protection software, online banking is the safer choice.

2. **Credit cards:** First and foremost, you should always keep your credit card and credit card account numbers in a safe place. Obviously, most people keep their credit card in their wallet or purse—which is why you should never leave these items unattended. Once a thief snatches

your wallet, he or she can rack up countless charges on your credit card.

Another way to protect your credit card is to order one that includes your picture. If someone else attempts to use your card, they'll be denied—unless, of course, the thief happens to be your evil twin.

You should also keep tabs on your credit card's expiration date and keep an eye out for the new card. "Be alert when a new card ought to be arriving," Frank writes. "If it doesn't arrive when you expect it, call the credit card issuer immediately and find out if the card was sent. If it was sent more than 10 days before your call, but you still haven't received it, cancel it at once."

3. **Debit cards:** Debit cards are convenient, but they can be extremely dangerous. There's a huge difference between credit cards and debit cards.

   The biggest distinction between credit and debit cards is that the Fair Credit Billing Act governs the use of credit cards. Under this act, if we let our credit card institution know quickly enough that we may be an identity theft victim, our liability is limited to just fifty dollars. But this law does not cover debit cards. Debit cards fall under the Electronic Funds Transfer Act.

   In my identity theft case, I had multiple businesses calling me saying that I had bounced checks. There wasn't much I could do about that. But had I been a victim of credit card theft and not check fraud, my exposure may have been limited to a mere fifty bucks.

Believe me, I can understand why many people prefer debit cards. They are convenient and easy to use. Plus, because debit charges are automatically withdrawn from your checking or savings account, you never receive a monthly bill. Not to mention there's zero interest.

But here's the problem: if you report a problem with your debit card within two days of the charge, you're just liable for $50. That's great—but guess what? The Electronic Funds Transfer Act (EFTA) says that if you don't let your bank know about a fraud incident within two days, you can be liable for up to $500. Beyond sixty days, your exposure is unlimited.

This is seriously bad news for a victim of debit card fraud. Obviously, debit cards are typically tied to checking accounts and savings accounts. That means that if the fraudster drains your savings account and you don't notice it within two months, your money is long gone. No one is going to replace it for you.

And it gets worse. Beyond the limits of your savings account, you may also be responsible for the overdraft charges under the EFTA. That means if an identity thief uses your debit card and drains your account, you'll also have to pay any overdraft line of credit charges. In other words, you'll be paying back money you never had in the first place.

It's time to get rid of that debit card. It may be

convenient, but it's way too risky. Tell your bank that you want just an ATM card that allows you to withdraw cash—not a debit card. Use a credit card to make your other purchases.

C = Computer

Because there are countless dangers lurking in our computers, we have to protect ourselves when we're online. "Only a relatively small percentage of identity theft occurs online, but you should take reasonable measures to protect yourself," the myFICO report states.

As part of your computer protection efforts, you should install a firewall, use antivirus and antispyware software, and antiphishing toolbars, and you should update all of these programs regularly. Never respond to e-mails requesting sensitive personal information, and do not click on links or attachments in e-mails from unknown senders.

The emergence of mobile devices and social media networks leaves us vulnerable to new threats which did not exist a decade ago.

Malware, spyware, scams, and cyber-exploits can be deterred and often prevented by installing and using regularly updated patches and sophisticated passwords, encryption and anti-virus software.

Refer back to chapter 3 for a refresher on specific computer protection techniques.

An Unbelievably Simple System

Protecting your identity is as simple as "Secure MIPC." In other words, secure your **m**ail, **i**dentifying information, **p**ayment tools, and **c**omputer.

I believe this simple system is the one of the easiest ways to remember what you need to do when it comes to protecting your identity. If you can commit the phrase "Secure my PC" to memory, you're golden. Just slightly change the spelling to "Secure MIPC."

Chapter 5 in a Nutshell

- Use the "home improvement strategy" to identity theft. Pay close attention to potential threats inside and outside of your home. The following common household items will remind you to protect yourself:

- Trash can: Shred all of your personal documents before throwing them in the trash. Dumpster diving is all too common.

- Front door: Be careful about whom you allow into your home—visitors can easily gain access to your sensitive data.

- Windows: Identity thieves are like Peeping Toms, always trying to sneak a peak at your personal information.

- Mailbox: Secure your incoming and outgoing mail, and opt out of unsolicited mail offers. Lose the red flag.

- Telephone: Do not give your personal information over the phone unless you are certain that you're talking to a trusted institution.

- Computer: Install a firewall and Internet security software to guard against online dangers.

- Safe: Keep personal documents locked away in a secure safe or a locked file cabinet.

- Washing machine: Steer clear of check-washing schemes with a Uni-Ball 207 pen—or don't use checks at all.

- Use this simple home improvement strategy to teach older family members and your children about identity theft.

- Remember that myFICO.com, a division of Fair Isaac Corporation, offers an effective identity theft prevention tool called "Secure MIPC." This is an easy way to remember how to thoroughly protect yourself from identity schemes.

- Mobile devices such as smartphones, flash drives, laptops and tablet computers can all be updated and protected from malware, rogueware, and spyware with the activation or purchase of anti-virus, encryption or tracking software. Check with the manufacturer for effective prevention measures.

Chapter 6
The Shocking Identities of Identity Thieves

*Lord, defend me from my friends; I
can account for my enemies.*
—Charles D'Hericault

When you imagine the face of an identity thief, who comes to mind? Does the label "fraudster" conjure up images of a shrewd, shadowy stranger? Do you think of an intimidating, hulking criminal who lurks in dark alleyways? Do you imagine a disheveled junkie dumpster diving for credit card applications hoping to scrape together enough cash for their next fix? Or do you picture an evil computer geek holed up in his dingy apartment hacking into websites and concocting phishing scams?

I have no doubt that more than a few identity thieves fit these descriptions. But the shocking truth is that the majority of identity thieves have extremely familiar, friendly faces. They are the faces of those you've come to know, trust, and love. In actuality, a large percentage of identity thieves are coworkers, friends, and even family members of their own victims.

"More often than not, identity thieves are friends or relatives of the victim who get their personal information offline—not electronically," according to myFICO.com, a division of Fair Isaac Corporation.

Speaking with the Enemy

Friends, coworkers, and family members are quite often the culprits! As unlikely as it seems, these people are often moonlighting as identity thieves—and they may choose to target you.

"Sadly, some identity thieves obtain in-home access to personal documents," writes Mari J. Frank in *Safeguard Your Identity*. "While we hate to think of those closest to us committing identity theft, it is more common than you might think."

I tell you this not to make you suspicious of every friend and loved one in your life or every domestic worker who enters your home. I don't want to turn you into a mistrusting paranoid who is constantly looking over your shoulder. I certainly don't want you to isolate yourself from all human contact in an effort to protect your personal information. That could get a bit lonely.

However, I think it's important to share this information with you because I want to help you defend yourself at every turn. If you hope to avoid the shadows of identity theft, you have to keep up your guard at all times.

More Shocking Statistics

I know what you're thinking. Your loyal friends and trustworthy coworkers would *never* do something as low-down and dirty as stealing your personal information for financial gain. And while you may have a few shady characters in the extended family like Cousin Eddie who did some time in the clink a few years back, he would never cause harm to one of his own relatives, right?

Well, don't take it from me. Just look at the statistics about the identities of identity thieves, as reported by Fair Isaac Corporation:

- A full 26 percent of identity thieves are friends, neighbors, and workers you allow in your home.
- Approximately 22 percent are family members and relatives.
- Another 20 percent are service employees, such as waiters and cashiers.
- Surprisingly, only 7 percent are online crooks.
- Approximately 6 percent are employees at a financial institution. (Although this is a relatively small percentage, it's a disturbing statistic nonetheless.)
- Another 4 percent of identity thieves are coworkers or other employees at the victim's workplace.
- The remaining 15 percent are others.[3]

---

3 Fair Isaac Corporation, *How To Prevent And Fight Identity Theft*, "Identity Theft and You," www.myfico.com/Downloads /Files/myFICO_IDTheft_Booklet.pdf (Dec. 10, 2009).

Additionally, Javelin Strategy & Research's revealing identity fraud survey report further proves that identity thieves are often friends, relatives, coworkers, or other acquaintances of their victims. According to the report, 53 percent of surveyed identity theft victims who knew the perpetrator's identity said that the thief was someone familiar to them.

The Javelin report states, "Contrary to what most consumers believe, in cases where the thief is identified, over half of the time the fraud perpetrator turns out to be a coworker, neighbor, in-home employee, friend, or family member. While some fraud is unavoidable, it is important to practice safe habits even in our own homes, for example, by not leaving sensitive financial information out where a new roommate can easily view it."

Welcome to Our Home

These alarming statistics go to show that the people you allow in your life and into your home are paramount to your safety. Unfortunately, with some of the blended and extended families many people have these days, unscrupulous family members may pose a threat to us.

It is sad but true that the roommates who live with us and the friends who visit our homes, are sometimes hiding a darker side. Also, there is a high probability that someone close to you is secretly in dire straits, but ashamed, unwilling, or unable to confide in you.

"They might be relatives or friends, roommates, household workers, home health-care providers, or spouses going through a divorce who hold a grudge," Mari Frank points out. "Worse yet, sons and daughters do this to elderly parents, and some parents steal the identities of their children."

When you do not properly protect your personal documents and sensitive data, you're basically offering up this information to any house visitors. If your mail is sitting out, if your PINs, passwords, and account numbers are not locked away, if your personal documents are lying around, you are making yourself vulnerable.

Any relatives, neighbors, friends, and workers that you may allow into your home can easily snatch your most sensitive, unsecured personal information. As you've learned in earlier chapters, these crafty thieves can unleash untold amounts of damage to you and your finances with even the smallest amount of personal data. Suddenly, you find yourself in the shadows of identity theft—at the hands of someone you know and thought you could trust.

This is why you have to remain vigilant of the people surrounding you at all times. Make every effort to shield your personal data from prying eyes and meddling hands.

The True Story of a Not-So-True Friend

In March of 2008, an Austin, Texas, television station reported that a thirty-six-year-old local woman was charged with stealing mail to commit identity theft. The thing is, she didn't just steal from strangers—she stole from her friends, as well.

One woman invited the criminal into her home many

times, considering her to be a close friend. The fraudster stole the driver license of the trusting woman's daughter and then used it to cash stolen checks.

The victim told the media she was "mad" and "hurt." I can only imagine the horror of discovering that someone you trusted and openly welcomed into your home had taken advantage of you.

This is just one of thousands upon thousands of similar stories. As a matter of fact, there are likely many more instances of this type of identity theft than we realize. That's because when some victims discover that a friend or relative stole their identity, they do not report them.

According to the Identity Theft Resource Center (ITRC), this can be an extremely distressing situation for the victim. When you personally know the individual who has used your information, the emotional impact of identity theft dramatically increases the sense of violation, betrayal, and embarrassment for yourself and the imposter. This abuse of trust can permanently impact your feelings about how you evaluate and relate to others.

What's Mine is Not Yours

So how do you protect yourself from the people you invite into your home without becoming a hermit who refuses all houseguests?

The aforementioned myFICO.com, a division of Fair Isaac Corporation, gives this advice: "Don't leave printed personal and/or financial information lying around at home. Keep checkbooks, social security information, billing information, and anything else a thief could use to steal your identity out of sight and secure."

As I've stressed repeatedly, you should also immediately shred any sensitive personal documents, including credit card offers and other junk mail, if you do not plan to keep them. If you want to hang on to some personal documents, file them away under lock and key, along with your account numbers, PINs, and passwords.

Don't put your personal information on display in your home. It's that simple.

Not-So-Friendly Encounters

Of course, the statistics show that identity thieves are not limited to the people you allow into your home. Oftentimes, it's those seemingly warm, genial people you encounter on a daily basis, such as waiters and cashiers. Those very people who so willingly assist you, offering service with a smile, may be scheming to swipe your personal information.

How does it happen? Think about it. You freely hand over your debit and credit cards to these people. What you may not realize is that servers and cashiers have the ability to palm little devices called "skimmers." With a single swipe of your card in this handy gadget, they have everything they need to create a counterfeit credit card in your name.

Deconstructing the Skimmer Scam

"A skimmer is one of the newest and much-prized toys on the frontlines of fraud," Abagnale writes in *The Art of the Steal*.

As small as a cell phone or a handheld PDA, a skimmer is a battery-powered, magnetic recording device. With one quick swipe of a credit card, the skimmer can read and store data from the card's magnetic strip, including the card number, the cardholder's name, and the verification code. The chip in most skimmers can hold information from up to three hundred credit or debit cards.

Skimmers are routinely attached undetectably to bank ATM machines, so be on the lookout for anything that doesn't look "right." Just walk away and report your concern as quickly as possible to local police.

Once the credit card information is stored in the skimmer, the fraudster can then download that data on a computer and e-mail it to other thieves throughout the world—for a fee, of course.

For the past few years, as this scam grew into a worldwide problem, card losses due to skimming surpassed $1 billion a year. Luckily, credit card companies and fraud investigators quickly caught onto this insidious skimming scheme. Over the past few years, law enforcement has been cracking down on the rampant crime.

For example, in April of 2007, thirteen people were indicted in a $3 million skimming ring in New York. The ringleaders recruited and managed waiters throughout forty restaurants in New York and elsewhere, providing each of the servers with a skimmer.

The participating waiters swiped patrons' credit cards through the skimmers and then passed the data onto the conspiracy leaders. The waiters earned $35–$50 for each credit card they swiped. The leaders then used the information to make $3 million worth of illegal purchases.

Luckily, credit card companies and investigators broke up this particular ring. The unfortunate reality is that skimming scams are not gone for good.

"Skimming is an immense problem," Abagnale writes. "With stolen credit cards, the criminal has a narrow time frame in which to make purchases, but with skimmed cards nobody knows these cards are out there until a victim gets his statement, which can be more than thirty days after the crime took place. That's a lot of time to rack up illegal charges."

Although you can't always maintain control over your credit card in a restaurant or store, it's critical to be aware of these types of scams. Stay alert and try to keep your eyes on your card after you hand it to a waiter or store clerk. Make it a habit to always examine your credit card bills closely upon receipt and immediately report any unauthorized or questionable charges.

Dodge the "Friendly" Arrows

Remember, you are a target, and those arrows are coming at you from all sides. Unfortunately, some blazing arrows wear familiar faces and pleasant smiles. These are the friends, relatives, house workers, cashiers, and waiters you think you can trust.

Oftentimes, these "familiar" identity criminals are the most dangerous kind, and they have the ability to do the most harm. That's because we typically relax and drop our guard around these people. After all, we would never suspect that our own friends, neighbors, or relatives would harm us. But as the statistics show, it is an extremely common scenario in the shadowy world of identity theft.

Don't ever let down your guard. It's so important to remain ever vigilant and shield yourself at all times. Even if you are in the company of coworkers, relatives, and friends, you still have to protect your personal data in every possible way.

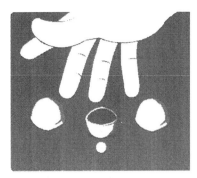

Chapter 6 in a Nutshell

- Statistics show that the vast majority of identity thieves are coworkers, friends, or relatives of the victim, as well as workers they allow in his or her home. These people can easily gain access to documents and personal information in your home.

- Never leave personal documents or financial information in clear view. Lock away check-books, social security information, billing information, and any other sensitive data.

- Waiters and cashiers are also common identity thieves. These crooks use handheld electronic "skimmers" to steal your credit card information.

- When you hand your credit card to a cashier or any other store employee, try to keep your eyes on the card until the transaction is complete.

- If you suspect suspicious activity with your credit card, report it immediately. Carefully scrutinize your credit card bills for unauthorized charges each month.

Chapter 7
Take Action!
A Step-by-Step Resolution Plan for Identity Theft Victims

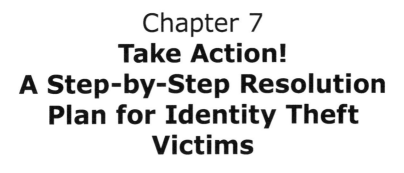

Action is the antidote to despair.
—Joan Baez

Picture this: as you are scanning your credit report, you suddenly stumble upon a suspicious account that you don't remember opening. Or let's say you start receiving threatening letters from an unfamiliar lender claiming that you are late on your loan payments. Or imagine that you keep getting phone calls from an angry department store representative who yells at you for bouncing checks you know you never wrote. These hints aren't very subtle, are they?

Quick—what do you do? Do you panic? Do you assume that the strange account on your credit report must be a misprint? Do you throw away the letters from the lender? Do you hang up on the department store collection rep?

Obviously, the answer to each of these questions is a resounding *no*. If you find yourself in any of these situations, you must take action immediately. Take it from someone who didn't act right away. If only I had followed my own advice, my nightmare may not have been quite as . . . well, nightmarish.

When I started receiving those angry phone calls from Nordstrom and others about the checks I'd supposedly bounced, I didn't take quick action. I just kept politely informing the collection department reps that they had made some sort of mistake. I guess I thought I could draw from my magician's skills, snap my fingers, and make the problem disappear. Of course, that didn't work out for me—and it won't work for you either.

When you start noticing the warning signs of identity theft, it is *never* an illusion. That suspicious account on your credit report, the letters from the unfamiliar lender, those calls about bounced checks—they are not tricks of the mind. They are absolutely real, and they will not go away until you take action.

When these warning signs emerge, your mind may try to convince you that everything is fine, that it's probably just some silly mistake, and you're being paranoid. But you'll have a gut feeling that something is not quite right—that there's something a little more ominous going on than a simple misprint. Follow your gut and take action right away. It could spell the difference between a minor situation that is resolved in a week or two and a major financial catastrophe that haunts you for years to come.

Know the Signs

I know I've covered this, but it's worth reviewing. According to the FTC, these are some of the warning signs that you may be a victim of identity theft:

- You receive information about accounts you didn't open or find debts on your current accounts that you can't explain.

- You discover fraudulent or inaccurate information on your credit reports, including accounts and personal information like your social security number, address, name or initials, and employers.

- You stop receiving bills or other regularly expected mail.

- You receive credit cards in the mail—even though you didn't apply for them.

- You are denied credit or offered less favorable credit terms—like a higher interest rate—for no apparent reason.

- You receive calls or letters from debt collectors or businesses about merchandise or services you didn't buy.

If any of this happens to you, it's time to take action.

Accepting the Inevitable

I hate to be the bearer of bad news—but the odds are that you or someone in your immediate family will become a victim of identity theft at some point. Every two seconds, another person falls victim, according to Gartner Research. As this chronic crime continues to spread throughout the nation, most of us are destined to come face-to-face with identity theft.

The good news is that if you follow a clear plan, you'll be able to more quickly resolve the situation if (or when) you become a victim. It is, after all, up to you to resolve your personal identity theft issues. No identity theft superhero is going to swoop in and save you. No magician is going to wave his wand over your credit report and make those unauthorized accounts disappear.

"Unfortunately, victims themselves are burdened with resolving the problem," Mari J. Frank writes. "No one can really take on this challenge for you entirely, not even a lawyer! You're the only one who knows your credit and financial picture, such as which are the fraudulent accounts and which are the actual accounts. So it's up to you act quickly and assertively to minimize the damage."

Baby Steps: A Step-By-Step Identity Theft Resolution Plan

Although each identity theft situation is absolutely unique, there are a few common measures every victim should take. If you think you've become a victim, you should immediately walk through the following six steps:

Step 1: File a police report.

This is essential—I didn't file a report when I was victimized, and in hindsight, I regret it greatly.

Contact your local police department as soon as you discover that you're a victim of identity theft. Although they may or may not be able to solve your case, filing a report will get you on the road to restoring your good name and repairing your credit rating. If police investigators are able to crack open the case, which they often do, terrific! If law enforcement captures just one more slithering slickster who has disturbed so many lives, it could have an enormously positive impact on public safety.

After you have notified the local police, you should also contact the police in the area where the theft might have occurred. For example, if you believe your personal information was stolen while you were traveling, contact the local police in the town where you think the crime went down.

Once you have filed a report with your local police, you should report the crime to one of the following agencies, depending on the type of theft that occurred:

Credit card theft: If your credit card or credit card number was stolen, be sure to contact the fraud department of your credit card company. (Read more on this in Step 3.)

Online identity theft: If you think your information may have been stolen online, you should notify the Internet Fraud Complaint Center at http://www.ic3.gov.

Stolen mail: If you suspect that your mail was stolen, report it the US Postal Inspection Service.

Call 1-877-876-2455 or file an online complaint at http://www.postalinspectors.uspis.gov.

ATM card: If the identity theft involved your debit card, you should report it to your local Secret Service office.

Step 2: Notify the major credit bureaus.

Contact at least one of the three major credit bureaus at the following numbers:

Equifax: 1-800-525-6285

Experian: 1-888-397-3742

TransUnion: 1-800-680-7289

If you call one of the credit bureaus, they are required to notify the other two. So there's no need to call all three unless it gives you peace of mind to do so.

When you call the credit bureau, explain your identity theft situation and request that they place a **fraud alert** on your credit report.

This tool is a great way to fight back in your own words, allowing creditors to hear your side of the story prior to rendering any decision regarding your credit status.

You should realize that there are two types of fraud alerts. First, there is an **initial alert**, which lasts only ninety days. The credit bureaus automatically place this type of alert on your accounts if you tell them that you *may* be a victim of identity theft. They also activate this type of alert if you think you could become a victim of identity theft in the near future—maybe because your wallet or social security card was stolen. When you place an initial alert on your accounts, you'll be entitled to receive one free credit report from each credit bureau.

There is an **extended alert**, which remains on your credit report for seven years. If you confirm that you are indeed a victim of identity theft, you should request an extended alert.

In order to place an extended alert on your accounts, you will have to provide one of the bureaus with an identity theft report from your local police department. Once the extended alert is activated, you will be entitled to receive two free credit reports from each of the credit bureaus within twelve months.

A **credit freeze** may be the solution for you if you do not intend to apply for credit anytime soon. A credit freeze prevents anyone from looking into your account to determine your credit worthiness. A credit freeze may not protect you from things like insurance fraud, employee/insider fraud, medical fraud, or data breaches.

In order for future creditors to view your credit profile, you will need to request a thaw. A credit freeze typically costs ten dollars for each of the three major credit bureaus, or thirty dollars for each freeze and thirty dollars for each thaw.

For more state-by-state information about freezing your credit, visit: http://www.worldprivacyforum. org/creditfreeze.

Step 3: Contact your creditors and respond to debt collectors.

Call all of your creditors, including your credit card companies, mortgage company, car loan company, and retailers where you have credit accounts. Let each of these companies know that you are a victim of identity theft.

If your credit card or account number has been stolen, ask the credit card company to close your account. They will issue you a new card with a different account number. If the criminal made charges on your credit card, your liability is limited to just fifty dollars by law—as long as you notify the credit card company in a timely manner.

If a fraudulent account has been opened in your name, notify the fraud department of the company where the account is held.

If you start receiving calls or letters from a debt collector regarding unauthorized accounts or false charges made to your actual accounts, respond immediately by phone and in writing. Tell them your situation, explain why you do not owe the money, and send them copies of your identity theft report or affidavit. You should also ask the debt collector for the contact information of the business trying to collect the debt and then contact that company directly.

Again, keep copies of your credit cards and other account information in one safe, secure place. If you become a victim, you'll need to access this critical information quickly so that you can make all the necessary phone calls.

Step 4: Take control of your bank accounts.

If you believe an identity thief has accessed your bank account, stolen your checks, or set up a bank account in your name, notify your bank immediately.

If your checkbook was stolen, ask your bank to put a stop payment on all of your checks and close the account. When you open a new account, make sure it is under a different account number. Also, have only your first initial and last name printed on your new checks. Do not include your social security number, address, or phone number on the check.

It is also a good idea not to reveal your gender or full name on your checks if initials seem sufficient.

If you think a fraudster is writing checks or has set up a fake account in your name, you'll want to notify the each of the following check-verification companies:

ChexSystems: 1-800-428-9623

CrossCheck: 1-800-843-0760

Check Rite: 1-800-766-2748

Equifax Check Services: 1-800-437-5120

TeleCheck: 1-800-366-2425

SCAN: 1-800-262-7771

These companies keep a database of check bouncers and may be able to confirm if bad checks are being written in your name. Some of them allow you to place a fraud alert on checks in your name. However, each of these companies follows a different set of procedures, so you'll have to call each one and find out what they require.

Step 5: Report the crime to the Federal Trade Commission.

Visit the FTC website at http://www.ftc.gov. This is the best site there is for identity theft victims. Not only can you report identity theft on the site, but it's also a great resource with all of the information a victim could possibly need.

The FTC strongly encourages consumers to submit fraud and identity theft complaints to their website. This helps law enforcement officers throughout the world keep tabs on identity thieves. It also allows the FTC to keep accurate statistics on identity theft in the nation—an important step to understanding and stamping out this crime.

Step 6: Create an identity theft affidavit.

It may take a while for you to figure out exactly what kind of identity theft has been committed against you and all of the specifics. However, once you have a better grasp on the details of your identity theft case, you should complete an identity theft affidavit.

An ID theft affidavit allows you to record a full description of your situation explaining what happened to you. You can then send copies of this affidavit to any debt collectors, credit bureaus, or credit companies asking for proof of the crime. You can obtain an ID affidavit from the identity theft section of the FTC website under "Tools for Victims."

"To make certain that you do not become responsible for any debts incurred by an identity thief, you must prove to each of the companies where accounts were opened in your name that you didn't create the debt," the FTC website explains. That's exactly what an identity theft affidavit helps you to do—clear your good name.

According to the FTC's website, "An official ID Theft Affidavit may be required for a variety of purposes, including to absolve you of the debt when an identity thief opens a new account in your name, or to obtain application or transaction records from a company the identity thief dealt with."

Unfortunately, not all companies will accept the same identity theft affidavit. Some institutions have very specific forms and paperwork that you will have to complete before they will supply you with the information you need.

"Before you send the affidavit, contact each company to find out if they accept it," the FTC advises. "If they do not accept the ID Theft Affidavit, ask them what information and/or documentation they require."

The FTC's ID Theft Affidavit can be found here: http://www.ftc.gov/bcp/edu/resources/forms/affidavit.pdf

Put it in Writing

As you plow through these identity-reparation steps, you're going to have many conversations with a variety of different businesses and institutions. Eventually, it will be difficult to keep track of or accurately recall who you talked to, when you spoke, and what information was discussed.

That's why you should keep thorough notes of every company or institution you call, including an overview of every conversation. Keep a clipboard or notebook with a log of each and every conversation, including dates, names, and phone numbers. This helps to avoid the panic and confusion that are commonplace when trying to resolve your issues with lenders, credit agencies, law enforcement, and others.

Be Proactive and Stick with the Plan

The key to resolving your identity theft ordeal as quickly and painlessly as possible is to be prepared *before* disaster strikes. Don't wait until you discover that strange account on your credit report. Don't put it off until you start receiving threatening phone calls from debt collectors. If you don't have a game plan before you actually become a victim, you'll find yourself stressed, confused, and uncertain where to turn. Put a plan together now while your head is clear.

Failing to plan means that you are planning to fail. A

little preparation now will make all of these steps much easier to take later on, should it come to that.

Make photocopies of all your credit cards and identifying documents. Include your driver's license, social security card, birth certificate, and even a business card. Keep all of this information locked up securely in your home or a safety deposit box so that you can easily access it if you become a victim.

Above all else, keep a copy of this step-by-step identity theft resolution plan handy in your home or office. With a strong plan, you'll be able to swiftly tackle the daunting task of clearing your good name if and when the time comes.

Chapter 7 in a Nutshell

- If you suspect that you are the victim of identity theft, take action immediately to minimize the consequences.

- Identity theft victims are responsible for clearing their own good name—no one else can fully take on this task for you.

- To resolve your identity theft problem, walk through the following steps:
  1. File a police report.
  2. Notify the three major credit bureaus (Equifax, Experian, and TransUnion). Consider the valuable benefits of a credit freeze and fraud alert.
  3. Contact your creditors and respond immediately to any debt collectors who contact you.
  4. If you believe an identity thief has or may gain access to your bank account, notify your bank immediately.
  5. Report the crime to the Federal Trade Commission.

6. Create an identity theft affidavit, including a full description of your situation. You can find an official ID theft affidavit at http://www.ftc.gov/bcp/edu/resources/forms/affidavit.pdf.

- Take thorough notes about all of the conversations you have with various institutions as you walk through these steps.

- Be proactive. Keep a copy of this step-by-step identity theft resolution plan in your home or office so that you can act quickly if you become a victim.

- Share a copy of this book with loved ones.

Chapter 8
Guarding Your Habit Habitat

*The real you is the person who knows exactly
where you wined and dined last night.*
—Peter Huber, writer and senior fellow
with the Manhattan Institute

People are a lot like snowflakes—no two are exactly alike. Each of us is truly one of a kind, defined by certain traits, characteristics, values, and interests.

Consequently, each individual lives in his or her own unique habitat. No, I'm not talking about an actual brick-and-mortar house—I'm speaking figuratively. I'm talking about a metaphorical residence that I like to call a "habit habitat."

Your distinctive habit habitat is built upon your unique blend of hobbies, interests, and, of course, your habits. In other words, you know where you like to be, to shop, to buy gifts, to spend your time and money. We each have a unique set of special places and habits in our "habit habitat."

Who's the Real You?

Over the years, I have accumulated my own personal habits and built up my own personal habit habitat. While I like to think of myself as unique and original, it is still possible for someone to counterfeit me.

The truth is that almost anyone can pretend to be me—or you—largely due to the anonymity of technology in general and the Internet in particular. "The Internet has irrevocably altered the nature of privacy and turned us into a culture of transparency," Abagnale writes in *The Art of the Steal*.

However, as Peter Huber says, the real me is the person who actually knows where I wined and dined last night. Huber is a distinguished writer and senior fellow of the Manhattan Institute, a think tank dedicated to developing and sharing new ideas about economic choice and responsibility.

"For the bank, the real you is the person who knows exactly where you wined and dined last night," Huber wrote in a Forbes magazine article entitled, "Secure I.D.s and the Net."

Huber goes on to say, "But the purveyor and price of last night's feast is just one more little record in your portfolio, and it too can fall into the wrong hands. The real you is much larger. It includes all the snapshots, all the different records that mirror your body or track your shopping, savings, debt, deeds, licenses, passports, birth and death."

In other words, *the real you* is defined by your habit habitat. But the real question is: Who's guarding *your* habitat?

Guard Duty

Because we are so vulnerable to those identity theft arrows, we have to carefully choose the guardians of our habit habitats. As you probably know, we can only protect ourselves up to a certain point.

Once our data leaves our grasp and falls into the hands of our banks or credit card companies, it's no longer under our control. It's up to these financial institutions to watch over our habit habitat—but it's up to us to choose wisely when selecting these guardians.

Your bank and credit card company should be familiar with your habits. They should be calling you when there is a sudden change or discrepancy in those habits. Are you receiving these "check-in" phone calls from the people who monitor your habit habitat from time to time? If not, you need to ask yourself why.

For example, does your credit card company ever call you and say something like "Are you in Atlanta? Suddenly, I'm seeing charges there although you live in LA. What's up with that?" I welcome those kinds of calls, and you should, too! I like to know that someone is always watching over my habit habitat.

If you never receive those kinds of calls from your bank or credit card company, they may be too big, too busy, or too distracted to effectively guard your habit habitat. If they are not calling you, find another financial institution that will.

You may want to try out a smaller bank, credit union, or financial services provider who actually cares about you and the safety of your habit habitat.

The Data Warehouse

Each of our habit habitats contains what I call a data warehouse. Within this detailed data warehouse, there's a wealth of information all about you.

The people who are the keepers of your personal information, such as your bank and your credit card company, are in the business of mining this data. They use algebraic equations and predictive analytics to determine if what you are doing corresponds with what you've done historically. These "miners" are the guardians of your habit habitat.

I know it may be a little creepy to think that someone is "mining" your data—but this is an extremely effective defense weapon against identity theft. We should all embrace this idea. The more closely our financial guardians watch over our habit habitat, the safer our identities will be from fraudsters. In the super-connected, high-speed digital world we live in, this is the best protection we have.

As we look to the future, we have to find ways to rely on partners to help us protect our identities—because we can't do it alone.

Porous Personal Data

Here's something else you may not realize—*your private and personal PINs, passwords, and preferences are **porous!***

What does that mean? Well, according to *The American Heritage Dictionary*, "porous" is defined as follows:

Porous (pôr´əs)

Adjective: 1. Full of or having pores. **2.** Admitting the passage of gas or liquid through pores or interstices. **3.** Easily crossed or penetrated.[4]

In other words, your personal data is full of holes and can be easily penetrated. This is particularly true if you keep all of your PINs, passwords, and preferences in one place. If you have all of this sensitive information in one repository, that repository is certain to be full of holes.

This might sound strange, but most observers agree that the passwords we utilize should be a lot like our underwear:

- Long enough (8 characters or more)
- Change them often
- Don't share them
- Don't leave them laying around
- Be mysterious!

Thanks to the insight of Mr. Peter Huber, I believe that we should consider farming out all that data to better protect to it. "In the age of digital networks, identity can be secured only by chopping it into pieces, storing the fragments in lots of different places, and continually updating and sharing them at Internet speed," he writes in his enlightening *Forbes* article.

---

4 Houghton Mifflin Harcourt Publishing Company, *Definition of "porous" at YourDictionary.com*, http://www.yourdictionary.com/porous (Dec. 9, 2010).

Some of that information resides on one server, and some of that data is stored on another. It may sound confusing or even frightening. You could lose yourself in the process of your data being broken up into numerous bits. But remember, when you connect the dots in your mind, the real you is the person who knows where you wined and dined last night. You can't lose the real you—but you can better protect the real you.

This is the future of the connected economy. Fragmented information in multiple databases brought together in digital speed is what now identifies the real you.

Predictive analytics utilizes statistical analysis to comb through data kept in many different storage banks. That data can be gathered to make predictions about everything, from your buying habits to your behavioral patterns. The data, mined from various sources, is often used to judge your credit, insurance, or employment worthiness.

Many of the commercial identity theft and credit monitoring services that are available in today's current cottage industry make simpler versions of these services part of their "protection" offerings.

Several identity-monitoring services claim to scour as many as 1,500 databases looking for the illegal sale or use of a client's social security number and other unique identifiers.

In the digital age, you have to choose the most watchful guardians to oversee your habit habitat and shield your identity. Don't entrust just anyone with your information. Find responsible protectors that have the power to confirm that the person presenting themselves as you is the real you and not the fake or manufactured you.

In other words, don't settle for a credit card company that never makes those "check-in" phone calls. If you're not receiving those calls, you're not being carefully guarded. It is time to choose a better protector.

Identity for Sale

Did you know that your habit habitat is an extremely desirable, informative, and valuable product? Your consumption habits and the habits of your family and loved ones are products that are constantly being bought and sold. Just ask Equifax, TransUnion, and other credit aggregators. Your purchases and often your impulse history *are valuable products for sale by data merchants.*

"Credit card companies are probably the best identity trackers around," Huber writes. "No surprise there—identity is an information product, sold for profit."

That's right—your habit habitat, including your name, address, birthdate, social security number, your buying habits, and all of your personal information are up for sale. Your personal information is bought and sold by credit bureaus, retailers, manufacturers, and commercial data brokers.

As a matter of fact, one particular information broker was embroiled in controversy back in 2005. Because there was quite a media frenzy surrounding the case, you may be familiar with the name of the broker: ChoicePoint.

ChoicePoint failed to confirm the identities of businesses requesting consumer data, as required by the Fair Credit Reporting Act. As a result, 163,000 consumer records were compromised, making these people vulnerable to identity theft. (Comforting, isn't it?)

Of course, ChoicePoint quickly cleaned up their act—after paying the price, big time. The data broker had to shell out $15 million in fines and settlement fees to resolve the situation.

Peddled Products

This just goes to show that we are not always in control of our habit habitats. As I like to say, your personal information and your habits are *products that privacy pirates peddle . . . perniciously.*

I know, that's a lot of *p*'s. (What can I say? I'm a big fan of alliteration.) But while this catchy phrase may seem silly, it's all too true. Your personal habit habitat is a marketable product that is up for sale.

So be very careful about who you choose to guard your habit. This is a world full of financial freedom—but as we know, with freedom comes great responsibility. Choose wisely.

The Guardians of Your Gate

Lyndon B. Johnson once said, "We did not choose to be the guardians of the gate, but there is no one else."

However, when it comes to the guardians of your identity, you *do* have a choice. I implore you to cautiously select the custodians of your habits. These custodians carefully control all the checkpoints of your buying habits and your life. Another way to remember this is something I call the Seven Cs.

The Seven Cs:

- **Carefully:** Use due caution and consideration.

- **Choose:** Don't procrastinate . . . do it!

- **Custodians:** There will be many keepers of your data—some known and authorized, some unknown and unauthorized.

- **Control:** Use it or lose it.

- **Checkpoints:** Guard the entry points into your personal world.

- **Composite:** There are many self-sufficient components that form a whole.

- **Character:** You are (financially speaking) most often who creditors *think* you are.

You have to *carefully choose* the financial *custodians* who *control* all of the *checkpoints* of your buying habits and your life because this is what makes up your *composite character.*

This is the composite you. This is the you that is broken up and distributed throughout multiple databases—when put back together is what defines your character. This is the real thing, the real you. It's the tree versus the shadow story from Abe Lincoln's quote that I mentioned back at the beginning of chapter 2.

Don't let just anyone keep watch over your tree—you have to carefully choose your guardians. Entrust your financial legacy only to those who can demonstrate a willingness—or, better yet, an *eagerness*—to carefully nurture, monitor, and defend your character and protect you from the shadows.

Chapter 8 in a Nutshell

- Each person lives in their own unique "habit habitat," made up of their special places, hobbies, interests, and habits. This habit habitat defines the *real* you.

- Your bank and credit card companies should be familiar with your habits, and they should call you when there is a sudden change or discrepancy in those habits. If this isn't happening, it's time to switch to a different financial institution.

- The guardians of your personal information often "mine" the data in your data warehouse to determine if your actions correspond with what you've done historically. This is an extremely effective defense weapon against identity theft.

- *Your private and personal PINs, passwords, and preferences are porous.* If you keep all of your nonpublic personal information in one place, your personal data remains full of holes and can be easily penetrated.

- Your habits are *products that privacy pirates peddle . . . perniciously.* Your personal information is bought and sold by the credit bureaus, retailers and manufacturers, commercial data brokers, and common thieves, as well.

- Because you are not always in control of your habit habitat, you have to be careful about who you choose to guard your habits.

- Remember the Seven Cs: you must *carefully choose* the *custodians* who *control* all of the *checkpoints* of your buying habits and your life because this is what makes up your *composite character.*

Chapter 9
A Long Walk to Financial Freedom

My long walk is not yet ended.
—Nelson Mandela

Now you are armed with some of the shocking statistics, a deeper understanding of the scope of this rampant crime, and some of the proven weapons needed to defend to yourself in the fight against identity theft and financial fraud. What do you do with this information?

I can only hope that you will use the techniques I have presented throughout these chapters to protect your personal data, staunchly defend your identity, and make yourself a smaller target. I hope that you will carefully choose the guardians of your habit habitat and remain ever mindful of those who hold the keys to your priceless personal data.

Do everything in your power to keep yourself and your family out those shadows of identity theft, and I hope that you will keep tabs on the real you. Remember—the real you is the person who knows where you wined and dined last night. The real you is, in fact, a healthy, flourishing tree with a complex network of strong roots binding you to the rich soil below.

The long-term concept of data security is flawed and elusive.

The continuum of reliable identification, multi-factored authentication and dependable authorization cannot be guaranteed secure by anyone.

The only currency with any lasting value in our evolving, portable, digital economy is trust.

Be courageous enough to follow your gut instincts, watch for those flashing alarm signals, and report any suspicious activities or discrepancies in your financial records. This seemingly insignificant commitment could ultimately save countless others from suffering at the hands of the same merciless thief.

After all, if you alert the authorities quickly enough, they may be able to take one or several of these financial fraudsters off the street and into early, permanent retirement.

A Collaborative Effort

Of course, consumers can only protect themselves to a certain extent. It will take the dedication and partnership of law enforcement, governmental agencies, various task forces, businesses, financial institutions, and lawmakers to truly stamp out identity theft.

Many governmental agencies, including the FTC, the US Department of Justice, the Department of the Treasury, the US Secret Service, the US Postal Inspection Service, and many others are fighting a tough fight against this rampant crime.

The identity theft scourge somehow continues to persist and spread. The anonymity of the Internet is a major contributing factor to this uptick in incidents worldwide.

This just goes to demonstrate how deeply entrenched that the enemy we're dealing with continues to be. Because identity theft is so widespread, so out of control, it will be no easy task to extinguish its flaming arrows.

The President's Identity Theft Task Force

One governmental group that is fully dedicated to stopping identity theft in its tracks is The President's Identity Theft Task Force. Established by executive order during the Bush administration in May 2006, the task force was charged with finding and implementing a new approach in the fight against identity theft.

According to the task force's website, "The President's charge was to craft a strategic plan aiming to make the federal government's efforts more effective and efficient in the areas of identity theft awareness, prevention, detection, and prosecution."

The President's Identity Theft Task Force truly seems up to the task of protecting American consumers. I encourage the curious to read their report entitled *Combating Identity Theft: A Strategic Plan* from cover to cover. Based on that report and as a former identity theft victim, I felt the government truly understood my dilemma. They really seem to grasp the concept of financial pain from the victim's point of view, and the focus of their agenda is to prosecute and punish the growing ranks of identity thieves.

The task force's overarching objectives are to:

- Secure our data
- Prevent misuse of our data
- Assist victims
- Prosecute and punish identity thieves

In order to accomplish these goals, the President's Identity Theft Task Force focused on three major areas: law enforcement, education, and government safeguards.

- **Law enforcement:** In the report, the task force presented information about the tools that law enforcement entities need to more effectively prevent and investigate identity theft crimes, prosecute the criminals, and recover the proceeds.

- **Education:** The task force examined how both government agencies and the private sector can educate our nation's citizens about how they can protect their identities.

- **Government safeguards:** As the task force website states, "Because government must help reduce, rather than exacerbate, incidents of identity theft, the Task Force worked with many federal agencies to determine how the government can increase safeguards to better secure the personal data that it and private businesses hold."

However, even the task force recognizes that this fight

will not be an easy one. "There is no magic bullet that will eradicate identity theft," they point out in the conclusion of their report. "Each of the stakeholders—consumers, business, and government—must fully and actively participate in this fight for us to succeed, and must stay attuned to emerging trends in order to adapt and respond to developing threats to consumer well-being."

Since the transition from George W. Bush to Barack Obama, President Obama's team remains watchful and vigilant on the cyber front during these desperate times. In 2009, the Obama administration declared our nation's cyber-infrastructure a "strategic asset" and has pledged to faithfully protect America's competitive advantage.

Closing the Curtain on the Magic Show

If only I could dust off my trusty magic wand, wave it around, and make this identity theft problem disappear. Unfortunately, it's not that easy. Part of the problem is that many identity thieves are talented "magicians" themselves. These unscrupulous scam artists are often employee insiders or trusted friends and family. Yes, it is frustrating and unfair, but reality can be harsh and eye opening.

Audiences witnessing the performances of theatrical masters of magic like Siegfried and Roy, David Copperfield, Lance Burton, David Blaine, or Criss Angel often yearn to know the "secret" behind the illusions. If laymen could discover the secret to their gambits, it would be like getting ushered backstage after the curtain drops.

That's precisely what these identity thieves do—they put on a flashy little show, but always from behind the curtain. Identity and financial fraudsters utilize clever diversion tactics or misdirection to throw us off their track.

"But scams aren't entertainment," as Frank Abagnale explains. "They gnaw at the fabric of society and ruin lives. We have to look at white-collar crime as being every bit as dangerous as armed robbery."

Many Miles to Go

I've said it so many times throughout this book, and I'll say it one final time. Identity theft is the fastest-growing crime in the United States. This financial crime is an epidemic, an all-consuming firestorm that continues to sweep the nation, due in large part to the portability of our data and the anonymity of the web.

As 2012 dawns and the presidential election looms on the horizon, energy prices are still unstable.

The lingering effects of the economic downturn continue to leave Americans gravely concerned about job creation, economic growth, the federal deficit, out of control government spending, and the rising cost of health care.

These are perilous financial times for many families. Other domestic and foreign policies trail behind our economic issues.

Over the past few years, our nation has made enormous cooperative strides and countless advances in the war on identity theft. We should be proud of our achievements, but we cannot stop now. We have come far, yet we still have many miles to go.

As we continue our journey to free this country from the clutches of identity theft and the future threat of global cybercrime, it's clear that the road ahead is certain to be a long one.

> *I have walked that long road to freedom. I have tried not to falter; I have made missteps along the way. But I have discovered the secret that after climbing a great hill, one only finds that there are many more hills to climb. I have taken a moment here to rest, to steal a view of the glorious vista that surrounds me, to look back on the distance I have come. But I can rest only for a moment, for with freedom comes responsibilities, and I dare not linger, for my long walk is not yet ended.*
>
> —Nelson Mandela

Chapter 9 in a Nutshell

- If you use the techniques I have presented throughout this book, you *will* make yourself a smaller identity theft target.

- Follow your gut. If you notice any suspicious activities or discrepancies in your financial records, report them immediately and follow the six resolution steps I presented in chapter 7.

- Because we can only protect ourselves to a certain extent, it will take a collaborative effort between law enforcement, governmental agencies, various task forces, businesses, financial institutions, and lawmakers to eradicate identity crimes.

- The President's Identity Theft Task Force is fully dedicated to fighting identity theft. The task force has focused on law enforcement, education, and government safeguards to help put an end to this crime. However, even this group admits that stamping out identity theft will not be an easy task.

- The anonymity of the web and the portability of personal data make it a challenging task to stem the tide of identity theft, data breaches, and financial fraud.

- Although our individual states and the nation as a whole have made many legislative, judicial, and technological advances in the war on identity theft, we still have many miles to go.

- The absolute security of our vital, private data is an illusion. Trust is the new currency.

Chapter 10
Identity Theft Resources

Credit Reporting Bureaus:

Most experts agree that if you discover that you have been victimized, your *first move* is to contact one of these major bureaus. By law, each is obligated to notify the others of your situation.

Equifax
PO Box 740241
Atlanta, GA 30374-0241
http://www.equifax.com
To report identity theft, contact the Fraud Division at 1-800-525-6285.
To order a credit report, visit their website or call 1-800-685-1111.

Experian
PO Box 9532
Allen, TX 75013
http://www.experian.com

To order a credit report, visit their website or call 1-888-397-3742.

To report identity theft, call the same number and ask for Experian Consumer Fraud Assistance.

TransUnion
PO Box 6790
Fullerton, CA 92834
http://www.transunion.com
To report identity theft, call the Fraud Victim Assistance Division at 1-800-680-7289.
To order a credit report, visit their website or call 1-800-888-4213.

Opt-Out Information:

To opt out of preapproved credit card offers from all three credit bureaus, call 1-888-5-OPTOUT (1-888-567-8688).

To prevent unwanted telemarketing calls, contact the Federal Trade Commission's National Do Not Call Registry at 1-888-382-1222 or http://www.donotcall.gov.

To drastically reduce the amount of junk mail flowing into your mailbox, contact these data brokers and request removal from their lists:

Database America
Compilation Department
470 Chestnut Ridge Road
Woodcliff, NJ 07677

Dun & Bradstreet
Customer Service
899 Eaton Ave.
Bethlehem, PA 18025

R. L. Polk & Co.
Name Deletion File
List Compilation Development
26955 Northwestern Highways
Southfield, MI 48034-4716

The Direct Marketing Association takes their time, but after about sixty days, you could see a reduction in the mountains of junk mail you must sift through on a daily basis. Write to them at:

Mail Preference Service
Direct Marketing Association
PO Box 643
Carmel, NY 10512

To reduce or eliminate *unwanted e-mail solicitations* from members of the DMA, visit http://www.dmaconsumers .org/consumers/optoutform_emps.shtml.

Government Agencies and Organizations:

Federal Trade Commission, Identity Theft
Clearinghouse
600 Pennsylvania Avenue NW
Washington, DC 20580

To report identity theft and find additional resources and guidance, call 1-877-IDTHEFT (1-877-438-4338) or visit http://www.consumer.gov/idtheft.

The Department of Justice

For identity theft information, visit http://www.usdoj .gov/criminal/fraud/websites/idtheft.html.

Federal Bureau of Investigation (FBI)

To report identity theft or fraud to the FBI, contact your local field office.

Visit http://www.fbi.gov/contact/fo/fo.htm for a listing of field office contact information.

Federal Trade Commission, Do Not Call Registry
To register your phone, call 1-888-382-1222 or visit http://www.donotcall.gov.

Note that you must call from the phone you want to register.

The Internet Crime Complaint Center (IC3)

A partnership between the FBI, the National White Collar Crime Center, and the Bureau of Justice Assistance, IC3 assists victims of cyber crimes.

To report a cyber crime, visit http://www.ic3.gov.

The President's Identity Theft Task Force
http://www.idtheft.gov

US Postal Inspection Service
Contact the US Postal Inspection Service to report stolen mail. Call 1-877-876-2455.

File online complaint at http://postalinspectors.uspis .gov/.

US Secret Service

To report ATM or debit card-related identity theft, contact your local Secret Service field office.

Visit http://www.treas.gov/usss/field_offices.shtml to find the field office in your area.

Check Verification Companies:

Check Rite
1-800-766-2748

ChexSystems
1-800-428-9623

CrossCheck
1-800-843-0760

Equifax Check Services
1-800-437-5120

SCAN
1-800-262-7771

TeleCheck
1-800-366-2425

Nonprofit Organizations and Educational Groups:

Privacy Rights Clearinghouse

This is a consumer organization dedicated to raising awareness and leading citizens to take action to control their own personal information.
http://www.privacyrights.org

Identity Theft Resource Center

This national nonprofit organization publishes studies, fights identity theft, and provides support for victims.
http://www.idtheftcenter.org

Mari J. Frank, Esq.

Mari Frank is an attorney, author, university professor, and a leading expert on identity theft and privacy issues.
http://www.identitytheft.org

The National Crime Prevention Council

The goal of this group is to reduce crime by helping citizens work individually and collectively with law enforcement. For nearly thirty years, the NCPC has impacted the media with public service announcements featuring McGruff, the Crime Dog.
http://www.ncpc.org

Consumers Union

This group publishes *Consumer Reports* magazine. Their mission is "to work for a fair, just, and safe marketplace for all consumers." This is a great resource for the latest news on security freeze laws in your state.
http://www.consumersunion.org

Major Credit Card Companies:

American Express

To report a lost or stolen card, call 1-800-528-4800.
http://www.americanexpress.com

Discover Card

To report a lost or stolen card, call 1-800-DISCOVER (800-347-2683).
http://www.discovercard.com

MasterCard

To report a lost or stolen card, call 1-800-627-8372.
http://www.mastercard.com

Visa

To report a lost or stolen card, call 1-800-847-2911.
http://www.visa.com

Identity Theft Loss Protection:

http://www.dalepenn.com

My website and blog provide ongoing, revised news about my speaking engagements, seminars, webinars, coaching and live-training events. The site also delivers valuable updates, resources, web links, support, and free gifts and bonuses for purchasers of this book. Type: *identitytheftsecretsbook* into the coupon code.

http://www.ipfc.us

The Institute for the Prevention of Financial Crimes was founded by former LAPD veteran detective Robert Rebhan. The IPFC is a leading US fraud prevention organization offering keynotes and workshops to educate businesses about issues of crime and financial control.

Free Credit Reports:

This is the only federally mandated free credit request site that isn't secretly trying to sell you something!

AnnualCreditReport.com

To order one free credit report per year from each credit bureau, visit http://www.annualcreditreport.com or call 1-877-322-8228.

State-by-State Credit and Security Freeze Information:

http://www.worldprivacyforum.org/creditfreeze.
html#statesecurityfreezelist
http://www.consumersunion.org

Alternative Web Browsers:

Firefox
Download for free at http://www.getfirefox.com.

Opera
Download for free at http://www.opera.com.

Chrome
Download for free at http://www.google.com/chrome

Bibliography

Abagnale, Frank W. *Catch Me If You Can: The Amazing True Story of the Most Extraordinary Liar in the History of Fun and Profit.* New York, NY: Broadway Books, 1980.

Abagnale, Frank W. *The Art of the Steal: How to Protect Yourself and Your Business from Fraud, America's #1 Crime.* New York, NY: Broadway Books, 2001.

"About the Task Force," IdTheft.gov. Accessed May 7, 2008, http://www.idtheft.gov/about.html.

"The Torn-Up Credit Card Application," Cockeyed.com. Cockerham, Rob. (2006, May 10.) Accessed February 19, 2008, http://www.cockeyed.com.

"Combating Identity Theft: A Strategic Plan," The President's Identity Theft Task Force. (April 2007.) http://www.idtheft.gov/reports/StategicPlan.pdf.

"Defend: Recover from Identity Theft," FTC .gov. Accessed March 6, 2008, http://www.ftc.gov/bcp/edu/microsites/idtheft/consumers/defend.html.

"Detect Identity Theft," FTC.gov. Accessed March 6, 2008, http://www.ftc.gov/bcp/edu/microsites/idtheft/consumers /detect.html.

"Deter: Minimize Your Risk," FTC.gov. Accessed March 6, 2008, http://www.ftc.gov/bcp/edu/microsites/idtheft /consumers/deter.html.

Frank, Mari J. *Complete Idiot's Guide To: Recovering From Identity Theft.* New York, NY: Alpha Books, 2010.

Frank, Mari J. *From Victim to Victor: A Step-by-Step Guide for Ending the Nightmare of Identity Theft.* Laguna Niguel, CA: Porpoise Press, 2004, 2005.

Frank, Mari J. *Safeguard Your Identity: Protect Yourself with a Personal Privacy Audit.* Laguna Niguel, CA: Porpoise Press, 2005.

"Secure I.D.s and the Net," www.forbes .com. Huber, Peter. (2007, August 13.) Accessed November 9, 2010, http://www.manhattaninstitute.org/html/miarticle.htm?id=4426.

Identity Theft: How to Protect Yourself Now," MyFico.com. Accessed March 25, 2008, http://www.myfico.com/crediteducation/idtheft.aspx.

"Identity Theft and You: How to Prevent and Fight Identity Theft," myFICO and Fair Isaac Corporation, 2006, http://www.myfico.com/downloads/files/myfico_idtheft_booklet.pdf.

Kirchheimer, Sid. *Scam-Proof Your Life: 377 Smart Ways to Protect You & Your Family from Ripoffs, Bogus Deals & Other Consumer Headaches.* New York, NY: Sterling, 2006.

PC Magazine, February 2008.

Smart Computing & Consumer Electronics, May 2008.

"Something Vishy: Beware of a New Online Scam," FBI.gov. (2007, February 23.) Accessed March 12, 2008, http://www.fbi.gov/page2/feb07/vishing022307.htm.

"Tools for Victims," FTC.gov. Accessed April 4, 2008, http://www.ftc.gov/bcp/edu/micro-sites/idtheft/tools.html.

"Working to Resolve Identity Theft," Identity Theft Resource Center. (2007, May 2.) Accessed March 25, 2008, http://www.idtheftcenter.org/artman2/publish/victim/index.shtml.

21st Century Dictionary of Quotations. New York, NY: Dell Publishing, 2008.

About the Author

Dale Penn reveals unique insights into modern identity theft, thanks to an unusual combination of insurance and risk management expertise, and many years as an award winning professional stage magician. He has packed this guide with tips, examples and checklists from lessons learned while overcoming his own personal identity theft ordeal. Dale is a busy conference speaker, corporate trainer and business coach. He lives with his wife and children in California.

Stay connected with Dale Penn

 BLOG | http://dalepenn.com

 TWITTER | http://twitter.com/dalepenn

 FACEBOOK | http://facebook.com/
thedalepenn

 LINKED IN | http://linkedin.com/in/
dalepenn

 EMAIL | dale@dalepenn.com

 SPEAKING /TRAINING/ COACHING |
http://dalepenn.com/speaking